PRAISE FOR STRESS AND THE CITY

"Are you one of the millions of people who have been downsized, divorced, or dumped into the wasteland of unemployment? You have to start over, but how can you pick yourself up and move on? This book reveals how taking two risks a day will change your luck and your life."

— **Oren Meiner**, international business consultant, Berlin, Germany.

"Suzanne takes us from the steps of 10 Downing Street in London, to zip-lining over the rainforest and being stranded in dangerous lion terrain in Africa. Whatever your fears – this book will inspire you to take a few risks and overcome them."

— **Andrés S. Vásquez**, Emmy award-winning cinematographer.

"Dealing with tough job interviews and sales presentations can induce panic and anxiety that feels like hitting the wall at high speed. Suzanne shows us how to handle those drop-dead moments and end up a winner every time."

— **Stephen Weigert**, retired race car driver and psychotherapist.

"Are you living with someone who you would describe as a dragon? And that's on a *good* day! While some relationships cannot be saved, others can. Suzanne's insightful and humorous stories show us how we can turn those dragons into darlings."

—**Mark Roseman** Ph.D., Founder of The Toby Center, Florida for families in transition

"Suzanne has mastered the art of writing with a warm and humorous style. You feel as if she is reaching out to you personally, not to the world in general."

—**Mark R. Levitt**, Professor of Advertising, School of Communications, Miami International University.

"This is a fun read. Suzanne's clever writing allows us to embrace all the good that can happen when we face our fears and experience the unexpected, exciting outcomes."

—**Mace Horoff**, Ted-X speaker & President of National Speakers Association, Florida

STRESS & THE CITY

THE POWER OF RISK-TAKING

TO TRANSFORM YOUR LIFE

SUZANNE ARNAUD ST.GEORGE,

N.M.T., C.R.S.S., C.H.C., C.H.T.

CHANGING THE WORLD ONE BOOK AT A TIME

This book was written to offer hope and inspiration to a million people around the world. When times are tough, let's encourage each other to take more risks and have more love, peace and harmony in our lives.

TABLE OF CONTENTS

"*Stress and the City*, like *Sex and the City* is fast-paced and funny and gives us fabulous tools to enjoy a happier, healthier and more exciting life."

CHAPTER 1

GOOD MORNING, PRIME MINISTER!

TAKING RISKS AT 10 DOWNING STREET

"You have to let go of who you were to become who you will be."
—Candace Bushnell, author of *Sex and the City*.

"Should I or shouldn't I take this scandalous risk? I need a sign, and I need it *now*," I screamed into the foggy London night air.

It was midnight on a freezing cold Friday in the city. The scandalous risk I was contemplating would change my life for better or *worse*. It was the kind of risk that could cost me my livelihood and land me in the Tower of London for acting like Bridget, in *Bridget Jones's Diary*.

"Suzanne's the black sheep of the family," my parents had repeatedly sighed despairingly. After this high-profile debacle, I wouldn't be holding my breath waiting for them to bail me out. They'd likely leave my risk-taking heels behind bars until I came to my senses.

My hands were shaking as I pulled a gold-embossed invitation from my purse. The gilt-edged envelope was addressed to the Prime Minister, Margaret Thatcher, at 10 Downing Street, not to *me*.

"Is this is how Guy Fawkes felt?" I asked out loud. "O lawdy, maybe I'm about to meet the same fate!"

Guy Fawkes, Britain's most infamous terrorist and a Yorkshire man like my father, had taken a *gigantic* risk when he tried to blow up the Houses of Parliament. Four hundred years later, every November 5th, Brits all over the world celebrate his risk-taking failures by burning effigies of him on their backyard bonfires. We even named the day after his demise.*

Clearly the British have very long memories. . . .

Was my life about to become a pile of ashes like Guy Fawkes? Would people laugh at me and say, "You shouldn't have taken such outrageous risks. Who do you think you are, hobnobbing with the PM? You should have played it safe and stayed with that sexy-looking man you married; at least you'd be financially secure!"

Six hours later, instead of lighting gunpowder in the Houses of Parliament, I lit up a pink Turkish cigarette in an attempt to steady my nerves. It didn't work! I drank two cups of strong Jamaican coffee, but that only increased my jitters. I had an overwhelming sense of fear and foreboding as I fumbled with my car keys, trying to unlock the driver's door.

I drove slowly toward Downing Street in my lipstick-red sports car. They say when your number is up, life flashes before your eyes. Nothing good was flashing before my eyes, only the number of speeding tickets I'd recently racked up, along with all my late-night feasts by the light of the refrigerator door.

It was only a short, thirty-minute drive, but with all my "bad deeds" coming back to haunt me, it felt like forever.

"O lawdy, is this really worth risking being hauled in front of a judge, losing my job, and landing in jail for the rest of my life?" I asked myself.

"Yes, of *course* it's worth it," I yelled, sounding braver than I felt. "How many people could say they visited Number 10 on *official business*?"

As if to accentuate my fears every traffic light I approached turned red. By the seventh red light, I began to panic! Was this a *warning* sign for me stop in my tracks and turn around?

O lawdy! What if the police mistook me for a blonde rebel bomber – or even worse, a disgruntled activist who drove fast German getaway cars?

Downing Street was the ultimate in drive-by risk-taking. Once I made the turn, there was no turning back.

After a long day of gut-wrenching, stomach-churning phone calls to local officials I'd been warned that any unauthorized person attempting to deliver a package to Number 10 would be hauled off to jail.

But the die had been cast! It was too late to change my mind! As I spun the white steering wheel of my classic convertible into Downing Street I was surrounded by British "bobbies."

"Time-sensitive document for the PM," I said, waving the envelope along with my ID in the air, but the police remained singularly unimpressed.

"Stop right there! Step out of the car *now*, Miss," I was ordered as I slammed on the brakes.

Every centimeter of the cream leather interior was inspected, followed by (almost) every centimeter of me. I was such a nervous wreck I dropped my keys *and* my purse and the contents spilled out all over the street. Would I have to explain why I had four hairclips, three lipsticks, and no handgun, I wondered?

Finally, I was escorted by a grinning policeman to the front door of Number Ten. I could tell he was thinking *she's really got guts.*

But the reality was quite the reverse! Not one solitary cell in my body felt gutsy. I was faking it until I made it to the front door without frothing at the mouth, or falling down in a panic-stricken heap.

The policeman ran up the steps ahead of me and knocked loudly. The door swung open. We were greeted by an elegant lady in a black business suit.

"I'm Mrs. Thatcher's secretary," she said smiling broadly as I handed her the invitation.

By now a crowd had gathered to watch me being hauled off to the Tower of London. Just when it seemed that I'd be spending the rest of my days in some dark dungeon, regretting these foolhardy risks, the policeman returned my ID and said, "Good luck to you, Miss."

I drove away in a state of shock. For a former scaredy-cat, this was a big stretch of my brand-new self-confidence. I wanted to tell the bobby that I was a beginner in this risk-taking business – but then I thought better of it. Like the Pink Panther, it was time to flee the scene before Scotland Yard arrived. . . .

Six months earlier I'd driven the same lipstick-red convertible through London's fashionable Harley Street. This day I was sobbing my heart out as I contemplated the gut-wrenching reprisals of taking another life-changing risk.

Taxi horns blared as scarlet double-decker buses spewed stinky exhaust fumes into the misty morning air, but my heart was so badly broken, I was oblivious to everything.

"What's to become of my lop-sided love relationship," I wondered? "Should I stay, or should I go?"

Both options had terrifying and potentially calamitous consequences.

For all of us, rich or poor, powerful or penniless, there's a tipping point! A point in our lives when we must sink and drown in our sorrows, or learn to swim.

After many years with a cold and controlling man my body had wasted away to a bag of bones. At a frail hundred pounds I was a mere shadow of my former happy-go-lucky self. I'd become subdued, sleepless, and socially isolated. I escaped my painful reality by stuffing my feelings down with food and then starving myself for days when my husband made derogatory remarks about my weight.

It was time to face the music. The music, in my case, was my good friend and mentor Dr. Benjamin an eminent psychologist with a client list that read like *Who's Who*.

I stepped from the cacophony of sounds in the street into his calm waiting room filled with floral-print chairs and copies of *The Financial Times*. The warm peridot-green walls were filled with photographs of European royals, race-horse jockeys, and rock stars. I was far too nervous to sit still, so I paced the hallway as I waited for his prognosis.

"Suzanne, you've reached your tipping point. You can't save your marriage; it's time to save yourself," Dr. Benjamin said softly. "Your weight is dropping every month, and you are much too fragile to continue like this. Your situation is already serious and if you can't gain a few pounds I'll have to admit you to a treatment center to ensure you stay alive.

"I telephoned your husband and asked him to join us today. I made it abundantly clear that if he didn't express some concern for you, and your marriage, I couldn't guarantee that either would survive. In my professional opinion, my dear, if you don't leave him soon you will die from a broken heart."*

While I trusted Dr. Benjamin implicitly, I wasn't ready for his *do or die* diagnosis.

"I need some time to think this over," I said, fighting back the tears.

"Time is of the essence here, Suzanne."

But it wasn't that easy. My family had threatened to disown me if I divorced, while my husband's family could make waves in my professional and social life. Doors that had been open to me when I was married would now be slammed in my face.

How could my fairy-tale love story have turned into such a heart-breaking nightmare? Yes, I'd fallen in love with one of London's most eligible bachelors. He was tall and handsome, with blond curly hair and a drop-dead gorgeous body. It was like a scene from the popular TV show *The Bachelor*, and yet out of all those lovely ladies, he had chosen me.

But behind closed doors, it was a different story.

My husband had a terrible temper which erupted whenever he drank. He would fly into a jealous rage if I wore anything that *he* considered too sexy or revealing. Worst of all, he would threaten me, if any man appeared too friendly toward me at a party or, God forbid, asked me to dance.

After years of being told that I was overweight, unattractive, and unlikely to succeed at anything, the sad reality was that I *believed* him.

In a society where a "stiff upper lip" prevails, the *only* thing my family cared about was keeping up appearances. It was easy for me to empathize with Princess Di, as we'd both been trapped in loveless marriages without a whiff of support from our nearest, and *not-so*-dearest.

I had reached my tipping point. If I didn't take a risk and start over, it appeared doubtful that I'd even *have* a future.

Decisions, decisions! It seemed I'd be damned if I did it, and dead if I didn't!

Stress engulfed every cell of my body as I left Dr. Benjamin's office. I gulped down the last dregs of my cold cappuccino, said a prayer for protection, and drove away from everything that was safe and secure, with nothing but the clothes on my back.

"How do I start over when my heart is broken, my bank account is empty, and my self-esteem has reached rock bottom?" I asked Dr. Benjamin forty-eight hours later.

"Take two risks and call me in the morning," he said with a big grin.

"You've got to be kidding?" I gasped. "I just took the biggest risk of my entire life. I need some rock-solid support, some tried and true advice, not this b@s#!"

"Most of us will stick with the hell we know rather than risk searching for our personal heaven. We prefer to play it safe and stay in a job we hate or a relationship that makes us unhappy.

"Despite what we are led to believe, life offers us plenty of second chances. Sadly, those second chances often show up at the wrong time, or in the wrong place. Instead of waiting for that fabulous lucky break, we can create our own luck and shift to a whole new level of consciousness by taking two risks a day.

"I'm not suggesting you act like James Bond and bungee jump from Tower Bridge, or steal the crown jewels. I'm prescribing a daily dose of fun and laughter. Taking two risks a day will change your life and your luck in expediential ways that are beyond your wildest dreams."

By now the room was spinning, and I was reeling from shock! I'd expected to be given *ten tips for starting over after losing all your money and your mate*, not this baloney!

"Now that I'm alone and broke, I need much more practical advice," I said, wondering what the hell I was going to do next. "As for risk taking, if I don't find a job, lickety-split, I'll risk losing my roof-top studio for failing to pay the rent."

Back in my studio, I spent the next couple of hours with my head in my hands, praying to make sense of this piece of crap advice.

Gill, a fellow artist, comforted me over the phone. "I've no idea how I'm going to survive financially. If I don't find a job ASAP, I'll be penniless *and* homeless."

Don't worry, Suzanne," said Gill. "I know this absolutely fabulous temp agency. They specialize in top-drawer temp jobs. You have the *right* BBC accent and the *right* education, and you know all the *right* people, so of course they will hire you.

"By the way, I hear they provide the culinary staff for the Queen's garden parties at Buckingham palace."

I crumpled to my knees as if I had been punched in the stomach! Instead of encouraging me, her words only *accentuated* my current impecunious status.

In my recent well-heeled past I'd been a fashionably dressed guest at royal horse races in Ascot and wedding receptions at the House of Lords.* Now, it seemed, I'd be lucky to get a job serving wine in the royal scullery, wearing a white frilly cap and apron.

Yes, it was a real-life *Upstairs, Downstairs* scenario, except that I was heading downstairs, instead of up!

It was time to face my harsh financial reality along with my first risk of the day. I stepped nervously into the snobbish temp agency, with all my fingers and toes crossed.

"Please God, let this interview go well," I whispered under my breath.

To my surprise, it went better than expected.

"We have a great temp job for you with a top-notch advertising agency," my interviewer explained. "You're articulate and creative and, by the way, you have the *perfect* look for this position."

Amazingly, my skinny, "bag of bones" look was considered very chic in the advertising world.

"This is a long-term temp job," he continued, grinning from ear to ear as if he had just discovered a diamond in the rough. "You will be working on some major campaigns and, by the way, they'll just *love* you."

In what seemed like the blink of an eye, my initial risk-taking had paid off with a totally unexpected benefit. I'd been offered a temporary job, where I'd get paid to be creative, in a work environment that was both caring and supportive.

My new boss was debonair and dashing – a Hugh Grant look-alike. "Suzanne, you're a great match for this job," he said with a big smile. Slowly but surely I was beginning to believe that I did have marketable talents and was *likeable* and, yes, maybe even *loveable*, after all.

"How's the risk-taking going?" Dr. Benjamin asked at our next appointment.

"I'm simply not convinced this works. Exactly how can two risks a day rebuild my self-confidence?"

"Most of my clients have given away their power. It doesn't matter whether they're rock singers, race-horse jockeys, or well-respected royals. Someone, usually a boss, parent, or boyfriend, has told them that they are not thin enough, beautiful enough, or doing enough. So they beat themselves up trying to do more and weigh less. The outcome is they end up sick, or in addiction.

"The next time you feel you're not thin enough, or attractive enough to be loved, use this. He handed me a hand-carved walking stick. Beat up a chair, a cushion, or a trash can instead of yourself!

"Risk-taking helps you take back the power you have given away and discover your true path in life. You're a gifted writer, teacher, and healer, and yet you gave all your power away to someone who didn't love you. Isn't it time you took it back?

Despite my misgivings, I scribbled my two daily risks and their outcomes in my journal. I shopped London's flea markets for upbeat, fashionable clothes, sampled bizarre-tasting foods, and joined an ashtanga yoga class that was frequented by professional dancers.

It was like a scene from *Sex and the City*. What little self-confidence I had regained was rapidly demolished by this sun-tanned, city slicker crowd. I was the only pale and flabby female in a room filled with 10 percent body fat, perfectly toned bodies.

Ashtanga yoga is like yoga aerobics. As a former yoga teacher I knew this was the fastest way for my body to heal and repair. According to my snooty classmates, I was an ashtanga disaster! I had to take deep calming breaths before each class so I wouldn't feel bullied by their obnoxious remarks.

My recovery depended on rebuilding my physical and emotional stamina, but my body remained frail and inflexible. It took weeks before I could make it past fifteen minutes of ashtanga yoga without collapsing on the floor, gasping for breath.

"Merde! If you're going to pass out in my class, please do it prettily," my sharp-tongued Canadian teacher pouted. "And unless you can sing, don't wear that yellow leotard again. You look like a bloody canary!"

After months of toil, sweat, and tears, along with professional recovery coaching* sessions, I rebuilt my physical stamina and recovered from my emotional eating disorder.

As to the long-term outcome of my two daily risks, it was, as promised, better than I'd expected. . . .

To my surprise, my Sloane Ranger boss offered me a full-time job, but I wasn't sure how to respond. It was a generous offer, but I hadn't taken this leap of faith to spend the rest of my life in a cramped city office. I wanted to return to my work in the healing arts and travel all over the world.

While my marriage had catapulted me into the lifestyle of a *material girl*, as Madonna would say, I'd quickly learned that money can't buy happiness. But what if I took a gigantic risk and followed my dreams? It would mean risking my safety as I traveled to work in dangerous locations and worrying constantly about making ends meet.

Was I physically and emotionally ready to handle these challenges? It seemed unlikely, so I hesitated. . . .

"I'll be gone for three weeks, so you'll have plenty of time to think about it," my boss said amiably. "I'm going to St. Lucia for a secret getaway with some *special* people."

Special people here meant – nod, nod, wink, wink – a politically inappropriate rendezvous with a member of the royal family, or a romantic tryst with a sexy movie star.

"I want you to organize a fabulous party to celebrate the success of our latest campaign," he added. "I'm leaving you in charge of all the arrangements while I'm gone." We were strolling toward his silver Rolls Royce as he tossed out last-minute instructions.

"Don't forget to double check the wine list, don't forget to have the invitations engraved, and whatever you do, *don't forget to invite Maggie.*"

This wasn't Maggie May, this was *Maggie Thatcher,* the PM, and of course I didn't need to ask for her address!

After months of taking two risks a day, a subtle change had taken place in my psyche. I'd shifted from being fearful of saying, doing, or wearing the wrong thing to become borderline *bold.*

"Can I hand deliver her invitation?" I asked coolly, as if I dropped in for tea at Number 10 on a daily basis.

He switched off the seductively purring engine and stared at me. I'd been offered this job because of my creative flair and impeccable references. My family's political and social affiliations had been scrutinized up the gazoo for several generations.

Just as he was about to leave me in charge, I was acting completely out of character. Instead of a well-bred Brit, I was acting like *Bridget Jones herself.*

"What *exactly* do you mean?" he asked.

"Can I hand deliver Mrs. Thatcher's invitation to Ten Downing Street?"

He threw back his head and roared with laughter. "If you do, this discussion never took place! Agreed? Good luck, Suzanne. I'll see you in three weeks."

Still chuckling, he jammed his foot on the accelerator and roared away, leaving me choking in a cloud of exhaust fumes.

"So was that a *yes*, or a *no*?"

The next forty-eight hours were a wild ride as I paced the floor fighting off waves of panic. Should I take this stupendous risk, which was like a lifetime of risks rolled into one, or should I be sensible and forget it?

And . . . what would Bridget Jones do? Would she take this risk or run for the hills?

You already know what happened next. . . .

Now here's the rest of the story. . . .

"How did you get away with it, *scot-free*?" my friends asked after I'd risked my freedom and my foreseeable future at Number Ten.

"*Scot-free*? What exactly does that mean?" I asked.

As a writer I'd read every English detective story from Conan Doyle's Sherlock Holmes to Agatha Christie's *Murder on the Orient Express*. Did it mean that while I'd escaped a humiliating grilling by Scotland

Yard's interrogation team, MI5 would show up at any moment and whisk me away?"

The day of the cocktail party arrived, and there was tension in the air. The lively chatter covered our successful campaign and our Prime Minister; but to my surprise it also included *me*.

"We heard about *you*," some VIPs remarked.

"Probably Interpol heard about my risky business, and by now my finger prints are plastered all over the globe," I laughed.

"Didn't the PM invite you in for tea?" a junior minister asked, jokingly.

"She knows where I am, so she's probably wondering what I'll get up to next," I replied.

"She's on her way, so you can tell her yourself," he said.

Sure enough, Mrs. T walked in on cue, while my stomach was doing flip-flops. I prayed fervently that the floor would open up and swallow me whole.

"I hear you're the adventurous type," said Mrs. Thatcher.

"Yes, Prime Minister," I said with as much confidence as I could muster.

"That's good! I like adventurous women," she replied.

Adventurous? Was she really referring to me?

Had the simple formula of two risks a day transformed me from anxious and self-conscious to adventurous and courageous? It was hard to believe, and yet this was how the most powerful lady in the land perceived me!

Four days later, Dr. Benjamin and I met for an elegant lunch of Scottish smoked salmon and capers at Harrods.

"I heard that your politically incorrect risk has thrown a spanner in the works and they've closed off access to Downing Street."

"Imagine that," I said, as we laughed together.

"What's my next step? I'm ready to make some changes. My job is wonderful, but I work late most nights, and socially I seem to be on everyone's *Do Not Call* list. I want to travel the world, become a successful writer, and have a loving, satisfying marriage.

"Mmmm, there's that *sex factor* again," he said with a big grin. "Sex, or more specifically the lack of it, seems to be the main topic on everyone's minds these days!

"Let's face it, Suzanne; your choice in men could hardly be described as *stellar*. I suggest putting sex and marriage on the back burner and focusing on your other two goals.

"Are you ready to take some more risks?" he asked.

"*More* risks?" I gasped.

"Stress in the city is caused by two critical factors. Did you know that 70 percent of the world's population lives in a city, and yet cities cover only 3 percent of the earth?* Living and working in these overcrowded conditions erodes our energy and exhausts our cognitive thinking.

"It's no surprise that over 50 percent of us have problems sleeping. We toss and turn, worrying how we can get from *where we are* to *where we want to be*. Despite our desire for change, most of us aren't willing to take a risk. The bottom line is we're scared that things will get worse rather than better.

"To get from where *you* are, to where *you* want to be requires taking three simple, life-changing risks.

Risk #1 – Write it down.
"Keep a daily, detailed journal of all the people, places, and things you want to see and do," he said.

"That doesn't sound very risky," I replied.

19

"You are taking back your power as you journal your goals and dreams. Most of my clients who have been in controlling or abusive relationships find that journaling surfaces deep-seated emotions of fear, anger, and frustration that can seem overwhelming.

Risk #2 – See it and feel it.

"Bring your journal to life by creating an Adventure Board.* Improvise by pasting pictures of the people and places you want to visit on your bathroom mirror. An Adventure Board requires action and energy, so play loud music and dance around in the buff as you imagine all your dreams coming true.

Risk #3 – Take action.

"Once a week spend a couple of hours developing your creative skills. You could try cooking classes, art classes, or dance classes. During your class, picture yourself making pastry in a French patisserie, painting on the Rialto Bridge in Venice, or dancing to jungle drums in Africa."

My Saturday cooking classes were packed with creative cuisine novices like me. Amidst cries, screams, and bursts of laughter our dishes went from dried-up and inedible to mouth-watering and delicious. As my sense of humor was revived, so were my hopes and dreams.

Eight weeks later I took another super-sized risk and applied for a job overseas. My initial interview would best be described as *disastrous* and I felt down and depressed for days.

"Be courageous," said Dr. Benjamin. "Continue building your creative skills, and never give up."

I had nothing to lose, so I took contemporary art classes and despite my fears of being laughed at, I exhibited my drawings at a local café.

After that titanic-sized risk, I was shocked when I was called back for a second interview for the job, and then a third.

At my sixth interview, with several hundred risks under my belt, to my astonishment, it seemed I was a viable candidate.

"We have three positions to fill. Could you be in Paris this weekend to meet with our associates?" I was asked. "If that goes well, would you be available to start work in Switzerland next month?"

Have you heard the expression, "the earth moved?" Certainly *my* little corner of the earth moved as I heard these words. Moments later my Adventure Board flashed before my eyes. Spending a weekend in Paris and learning to ski were two images I'd glued to my bathroom mirror and danced around in the buff.

After a stressful meeting in Paris, where I was offered a job, followed by a week of sleepless nights when I was worried sick, I *still* couldn't make up my mind. Should I accept their offer, or stick with my safe city job and limited social life in London?

Exhausted from lack of sleep, I needed some emotional support from my friends. Over a roast beef dinner in a rustic eighteenth-century wine cellar, surrounded by racks of wine and seasoned oak barrels, I described my career dilemma. But instead of being thrilled about my job offer overseas, they appeared critical and judgmental.

"I don't get it," said Bodisha, a talented fashion designer. "Surely your family, or your ex, could help you out financially, so you wouldn't have to swan off to Switzerland to work?"

"I gave up a lot so that I could live in *integrity*," I replied.

"You could be on the edge of glory, or the edge of defeat," said Henri, a script writer and my out-of-shape tennis partner. While his dream was to play at Wimbledon, I didn't need a crystal ball to know this would take a bolt-of-lightning miracle.

Was I crazy to think that my run of good fortune would continue, I wondered? What if I accepted the job in Switzerland and then hated it? Or even worse, what if they hated *me*, and sent me packing?

"I feel I've made no progress," I sobbed in Dr. Benjamin's office. I simply can't make a decision. "Should I take a calculated risk and accept the job in Switzerland, or stay put?"

"Taking big risks means acting in *your* best interests, rather than anyone else's. While working in Switzerland feels like a leg up for you, it can feel like a letdown to your creative friends.

"There are no guarantees when we choose our careers and love partners. Your move to Switzerland could be an absolutely fabulous success, or a total fiasco.

"Whatever you decide – remember this. Don't get to the end of your life and have regrets that you lived other people's dreams rather than your own."

They say when one door closes another one opens. This was a year when I'd seen a dozen doors close and stay locked and bolted.

The man I'd loved for many years made no attempt to repair our fractured relationship. He ignored Dr. Benjamin's phone calls and letters requesting a meeting to resolve our issues.

My posh friends, who had promised to stick by me, had quickly crossed me off their dinner party list as the impecunious, almost divorced wallflower.

My artistic contemporaries thought I was crazy to leave a safe, creative job and move to a country where I had no friends, or family, and I spoke imperfect French.

After crying a bucketful of tears, it was time to take my next big risk and not look back with regrets.

23

If risk-taking, creativity, and courage were the keys to finding my true purpose and passion in life, I'd already wasted enough time. . . .

LIFE-CHANGING RISKS AND REWARDS

#1 Learning to take risks.

Are you feeling stressed and anxious as you read this? I can certainly relate! Did you lose your job, your home, or the love of your life? Has your whole world just fallen apart? If so, it's time to give yourself a twenty-four hour makeover!

A survey in the British newspaper *The Union Jack* found that Brits moan for seventy-two hours every year. I'm sure this survey was taken by some highly optimistic Brits who spend their winters in the warm, sunshiny days of southern California rather than the cold and snowy days of a Scottish winter.

OK, OK, I know some of you are protesting that you *never complain*. Don't worry, the rest of us are making up for you!

If you are not a complainer, you've probably read my first book, *Do You Dread Monday mornings? How to Be Resilient in a Stress-filled World.** It is jam packed with hilarious true stories about taking a positive and pro-active approach to life, especially on Mondays!

Let's say on average we spend one hour a day, or 365 hours a year grumbling on the phone, on the freeway, and with our long-suffering family and friends.

Imagine what you could do with that time! You could write a book, start your own business, or become fluent in Mandarin or French.

But what if you have a longed-for dream to fulfill? In less than one year you could take 700 risks and become a fully fledged adventurer in life.

Here's what it takes. . . .

"Twenty seconds of insane courage," says Matt Damon in the movie *We Bought a Zoo.*

Yes, you *can* summon up twenty seconds of courage. And yes, it's good for your heart and soul to experience fun and excitement, even if it's just for twenty seconds, twice a day.

Instead of stewing over past mistakes, why not spend the same amount of time taking two risks today? Start by taking *only* fun-filled risks. Wear a brightly colored shirt to work, sample some octopus sushi, or smile at complete strangers.

Now, take another risk and refuse to complain about *anything* – not even the *weather* – for the next twenty-four hours!

It's *amazing* how different you will feel.

Take two risks and call me in the morning has been my mantra since my first day, living solo, in the city of London. Like the TV show, *Sex and the City*, risk-taking works best when you share your adventures with friends. Call a friend every day and laugh over your fun-filled, bodacious risks, as well as those embarrassing moments.

#2 Transformation is an inside job.
Many of us, for a variety of reasons, have allowed our parents, bosses, or spouses to define who we are and how we should live our lives.

Chances are this definition doesn't fit you anymore. Are you ready to change that definition and live in integrity? Yes, you *can* reinvent yourself as a courageous and self-confident person by following the same simple tips that turned my life around.

If you *don't* want to put up with any more put-downs, try these natural Bach flower remedies.*

Centaury: If you are in a controlling relationship, or you work for an overly critical boss, Centaury will help you set clearer, safer, boundaries so that your personal needs are not constantly stepped on. If you are ready to say, "I'm not going to take this anymore," you are ready to take Centaury.

Walnut: a great remedy for coping with major changes in life, such as changing jobs, homes, or love partners. If you feel emotionally drained as a result of unprecedented changes, Walnut will subtly calm these roller-coaster emotions.

#3 Discover your Sense of Style.

You don't have to be bound by the mistakes of the past. If you've been stepped on, or are still being stepped on, your self-worth has been diminished. Here's the risk that helped me the most.

Today, start moving from where you are toward where you want to be by dressing up.

Why not give people something to like about you? When you dress up they will say "You look good today. I like that shirt," "that scarf," or "that fluffy sweater."

Style doesn't require big bucks. Shop vintage shops and consignment stores for your new look. Have a clothes swap party and ask your friends to bring clothes to swap. Swapping clothes helps you find your personal sense of style, and best of all it's free.

How you feel when you look in the mirror affects how your day will unfold. Why not make this your *most* important risk of the day – to always walk out the door wearing something that makes you look and feel fabulous?

If someone makes a snippy remark, remember this: 10 percent of the world is unreasonable and *unpleaseable*. No matter what you wear, they will always find something to criticize.

Dress up, and not only will you feel better and stand taller, people who have stepped on you, will step back. . . .

#4 Act bolder and braver by using props.

Did you know you can be bolder and braver in the blink of an eye? Actors use props to emphasize their script and boost their self-confidence. It doesn't matter how anxious you feel today; you *can* boost your self-confidence by using doorways as props.

How many doors do you go through each day? Hundreds if you count cars, stores, and office doors! Instead of saying "I don't know if this will work," which simply guarantees it will not, why not see each new door as a sign of better luck, and better times ahead?

Act as if you are bold and brave each time you step through a doorway. Boost your confidence a notch higher by saying or singing a one-line script and give it your best Oscar-winning performance. . . .

New doors are opening for me every single day.

Amazingly, it works!

#5 Opportunity vs. danger.

Before we start on our risk-taking adventures, we must learn to differentiate between risks that move us forward in life and those that hold us back or harm us. If you've already started down a new path, chances are you've been through some life-changing experience, or crisis.

In Chinese, the word *crisis* is written with two symbols. One symbol means danger and the other means opportunity.

Your two daily risks are like this. Every risk we take gives us an opportunity to expand our world from the same old, same old to something new and different. At the same time, each risk carries some danger that we'll look foolish, or even stupid.

What if we refuse to take risks and play it safe? Opportunities will pass us by on the conveyor belt of life that will never come around again.

Be assured, this book is *not* about flirting with danger or putting your life on the line. It's about putting your spirit of adventure on the line and seizing any golden opportunities that come your way.

#6 Finding purpose in senseless situations.

How long have you been searching for ways to transform your life and make a fresh start? Ten years, twenty years, thirty years, or even longer? It really doesn't matter. You were not born with a date stamp on your derriere saying *Use by this expiration date,* or it's too late.

Starting over has no expiration date or age limit!

In *Life Expectancy: It's Never Too Late to Change Your Game* William Keiper reviews a study of ninety-five-year-olds. When asked what they would do if they could turn back the clock ten, twenty, or more years, they all agreed they would take more risks. Even at age eighty-five, they believed that their lives would have been more fulfilling if they'd been willing to take a few risks.

Why wait till age eighty-five to recognize that taking risks is the key to a more fulfilling life?

Most of us at a turning point in our lives will beat ourselves up over our past bad choices. This negative mental chatter wears down our resolve to change. It's those *why bother* thoughts that swiftly erode our hopes and dreams of making a fresh start.

If you are going to talk to yourself anyway, why not say something nice? Take a risk and say, "Every day, in every way, I'm getting better and better."

One hundred years ago, Émile Coué, a French psychologist, astounded Paris by asking his patients to say" *Every day, in every way, I'm getting better and better.*" Can you guess the outcome? Yes, they all got better!

What we say to ourselves *matters*. It matters more than I can explain in words. When you say this phrase out loud throughout your day, you will see for yourself how ten little words can change your life.

If you wait until *times* get better, you could be waiting for the rest of your life.

#7 Take your first risk today.

Most of us are led to believe that the cosmic deck dealt us an ordinary, run-of-the-mill hand. So we live each day with an expectation that our lives will always be – ordinary and run-of-the-mill.

Here's the most important lesson I learned from daily risk-taking: Fulfilling a dream of happiness has little to do with the cards we've been dealt.

The real deal is this: Are *you* willing to take a risk and shuffle the deck?

If you've been blessed with good genes, eat a healthy diet, exercise regularly, and have discovered how to detox your body and reduce your stress, you can live 30,000 days, or eighty-five years and beyond.**

"30,000 days! That's so little time!" you are probably gasping. "How many days do I have left based on that formula?" Doing the math can catapult you off the couch and into action.

Take heart! It really doesn't matter whether we're given a long or short life, or whether we're dealt a good or bad hand from the get-go. At any given moment, we can say, "I'm ready to take a few risks, shuffle the deck, and take another shot at finding happiness."

The moment we make this decision, and start taking small daily risks, the only question we'll find ourselves asking is this:

"Why didn't I do this sooner?"

*See References and Research
**See Anti-Aging Secrets p.199

CHAPTER 2

YOU LOST THE JOB AT "HELLO."

"When we are no longer able to change a situation, we are challenged to change ourselves." —Viktor Frankl

Has it ever occurred to you that "Hello" is just "Hell" with an "o" on the end of it?

Like it or hate it, in these challenging economic times, most of us will have to take a risk and say, "Hello," to a brand new career. Whether this means selling a new product or selling ourselves to a new employer, the same winning skills apply.

The first thing you should ask yourself is, "How will people react when I say "Hello?"

Will they be smiling and saying a warm "Hello" back, or will they be inwardly groaning, "O hell. Oh no!"?

In less than 10 seconds, the person you are greeting will have made a snap decision about you, based on your body language and the way you present yourself.

First impressions are lasting impressions. Here are a few things you should know before you shake hands. . .

It was six o'clock on a damp and dreary Monday morning in the city of London. I was ready to leave the rain and sleet of a seemingly endless English winter for the snow-capped mountains and bright, sunshiny days of southern Switzerland.

My posh city friends had finally stopped telling me how I should, or could, have better handled the maelstrom of my marriage. The day I announced that I was leaving for Switzerland with a crisp, triple-signed contract in my hand, their attitude changed.

"Well, it looks like it's all going to work out for the best," they commented. "You've been offered a creative job in Switzerland. That's amazing! We *really* underestimated your talents."

From my perspective, I didn't feel *nearly* so smart or successful. After all, I was brand new to this risk-taking business. Moving to another country, all alone, felt like the type of bodacious risk only Bridget Jones would take!

My fingers and toes were tightly crossed during the flight, just in case my marketable talents disappeared once I left the White Cliffs of Dover. To make matters worse, our flight path over the Alps was rough and bumpy, which did nothing to ease the acid churning and burning in my stomach. As I staggered off the British Airways jumbo jet, my head was buzzing and my knees were knocking from new-job nerves.

"My job will be better than expected," I told myself, and then I quickly added, "From my lips to God's ears."

It was the first day of my brand new career in Switzerland. I was excited, thrilled, and terrified, all at the same time.

I had finally arrived. Or had I . . . ?

I spun around in the shiny, revolving glass doors that made me feel dizzy *before* I'd stepped inside my new corporate offices. My feet sank into carpet so soft, it felt as if I were floating on air.

"Bonjour," I said as I handed my business card to the receptionist, who wrinkled her nose and took it with her fingertips as if it were medically contaminated material.

"Herr Schneider waits now to interview you," she said snootily in broken English.

"*Interview me?*" I said in a startled voice. "But I already interviewed six times in London, and signed a binding contract before I left."

"Herr Schneider sees you *now*. This way please," the receptionist said sharply.

I had expected a warm welcome and "Thanks for traveling all the way from London to work with us." Nein, nein, liebchen! Herr Schneider resembled a British bulldog that hadn't been fed for days. He growled a husky "Hello" and barked a few words in Swiss-German to his assistant, who shot me a sympathetic look and fled the room.

"So, I received your résumé," he snapped, as he swept his hand over my C.V. as if it were some worthless piece of paper.

"This is not looking good," I muttered. I had two suitcases in my tiny hotel room, and no return ticket home.

I smiled, and elected to at least *act as if* I were the capable and confident professional they had hired over a thousand miles away.

"Do you speak French?" he asked, without looking up at me.

"Yes, sir," I said, thinking this would be a good time to start groveling.

"Do you speak German?" he snapped.

"Yes, sir, at a conversational level, but I'm not fluent," I replied.

Herr Schneider glared at me, and his beady eyes were now glittering! After a long, fierce stare, he sucked air loudly through his shiny silver teeth as a sign of extreme displeasure.

"Do you speak *Italian*?" he barked.

"*Italian*?" I asked incredulously. No one had asked me this question in six prior interviews.

"No, sir," I said, wondering if I was about to be fired before I'd even started this job.

Herr Schneider leapt to his feet, but this time he was snarling. His resemblance to a bulldog was growing stronger by the minute.

"This is Ticino. Our clients speak Italian, and our staff speaks Italian. You learn to speak Italian, or you're no good to me, and I send you *home*," he roared. "I'll give you one month. Go, go," he said, waving his hand toward the door, indicating that I should run out the door and learn Italian – instantly!

Some companies offer incentive plans. I had been offered the *ultimate* incentive plan: Speak Italian, or be sent packing. My heart was pounding as I left his office. I was now facing the humiliating prospect of having to limp back to London with my tail between my legs.

In the past year I'd been snubbed by several of my society friends and their families. Sad to say, when you divorce, your family and friends will take sides – and the side that they take can surprise you. They are not looking out for *you*; they are looking out for *themselves*.

Sometimes, the people you care about the most will desert you. Instead they'll stick like superglue to whoever has the most power and influence. And, let's face it, in my divorce that would *not* be me.

Talk about adding insult to injury. It was bad enough being rejected by my nearest and not-so-dearest. Now I was facing the harrowing prospect of being rejected by my brand new boss, before I'd been given a chance to prove myself.

"What happened?" everyone would ask as I crawled ignominiously back to London.

"I was fired because I couldn't speak Italian," I'd be forced to admit.

"I just *knew* it. She's just not tough enough to handle the international job market. She should have kept a stiff upper lip and stayed with that frightfully boring man she married," they would whisper behind my back, like some posh party scene in *Pride and Prejudice.**

Twenty-four hours earlier, I'd risked leaving a job that was safe and secure to start a new venture in Switzerland. But this was no fairy tale; this was rapidly turning into a Steven King *horror* story. I was learning the hard way that the Swiss work ethic was much tougher than I'd been accustomed to. Worst of all, my job security was hanging by a thread that could snap at any moment. . . .

How could this critical piece of information have been overlooked? After all, I'd been subjected to six high-stress interviews – where questions were fired at me in rapid succession – only to be sweating bullets after I'd triple-signed a contract and traveled to another country a thousand miles away!

"Someone's head is about to roll over this," I sobbed, and then quickly realized that the *someone* in this scenario was likely to be me. . . .

Was my career move turning into the humiliating fiasco that Dr. Benjamin had warned me about? Waves of panic swept through my body as after dozens of attempts to reach him, I gave up.

"OK plan B didn't work, so I'll have to go with plan C – the crisis plan."

Despite my mother's prima donna attitude, I threw caution to the wind and phoned home.

As I was telling my grueling interview story, there was a stony silence at the other end of the phone, like *nobody's home*. I waited for some sounds of sympathy, but she didn't say a word.

Surely, the phone line must have gone dead!

"Hello, hello, are you still there?" I asked, as I tapped my phone to make sure it was still working.

When my mother finally spoke, it was a crisp one-liner: "Just do it, Suzanne."

"Do *what?*" I asked.

"Learn to speak Italian," she said haughtily, as if she were giving a Nike commercial for Italian.

"If I can *sing* in Italian, you can certainly learn to *speak it.*"

As an opera singer, my mother had performed dozens of operas in Italian. While she had a valid point, it felt more like a bitter pill I was being forced to swallow.

"You have only two choices here," my mother continued in a sharp staccato tone. "You can spend the next month feeling sorry for yourself and get fired, or you can pull yourself up by your bootstraps and act like a winner instead of a whiner."

What did I do? How did I cope? Truthfully, I wanted to throw in the towel and run away from these impossible demands and language challenges. Fortunately, I had burned *all* my bridges. I say *fortunately* because once you've cut all lines of retreat, there's no going back; you can only go forward.

So instead of running, I put on my risk-taking hat and went to work.

I spent the next thirty days struggling to converse with my co-workers in wretched Italian and the next thirty nights studying at a local language school. After drinking enough cappuccino to keep the entire city awake, I learned enough Italian to keep my job.

Working in Switzerland was both a humbling and an enlightening experience.

Most Swiss nationals speak four languages fluently. As a Brit who only spoke English well – and the rest very shabbily – I was the target of many jibes and jokes. After dozens of embarrassing moments as I struggled to converse in Italian, I acquired many new friends along with considerable respect from my employer.

Don't get me wrong; my life wasn't *all* work and no play. Far from it!

Even though I am terrified of heights, I decided to challenge my fears and take skiing lessons. For me, learning to ski in the Swiss Alps was like standing on the roof of a hundred-story building, staring into the snowy abyss and questioning my *sanity*, while Gino, my handsome Italian ski instructor, yelled "Go, go, go, Susanna."

Thank you God were the words that popped into my head the day I met Gino. Maybe he'd be my *sexiest* incentive to learn Italian.

"No, no, I can't go. I'm scared, Gino! Let me stay on the baby slopes till I can build up my confidence!"

Fortunately for me, Gino was handsome *and* kindhearted. He helped me face down my fears both on the slopes and off. But that's a story for another book. . . .

As for my adventures on the slopes, forget those glamorous images you've seen of Olympic athletes, skiing the slopes in their elegant ensembles. I spent more time slithering on my butt in the snow than upright on my skis. And somehow I never managed to look "cool" leaping for that long, slippery pole that is euphemistically called a ski lift.

While I don't believe in seeking revenge, I have to admit it was spine tingling, letting slip to a gossip columnist, who had snubbed me after my divorce, that I was dating a handsome ski instructor. This would be like the second coming of the Great Fire of London as my story burned up the phone lines in the city. Sooner or later, it would reach the ears of my ex-husband.

After years of being told that I was overweight, unattractive, and unlovable, it was highly entertaining to imagine his expression when he heard this news.

Here's some good news for you. If you're ready to take a risk and try something new, you don't have to be an expert or even be *good* at it to experience endless fun and laughter. If it's a new sport you're learning, then you'll end up with some bruises and a sore butt. If it's a new language, then you'll probably embarrass yourself by saying something stupid. In the long run, the ache of inertia and not giving it your best shot will be much worse than any temporary soreness or shame.

One year later, I left Switzerland for a new job in Denmark feeling exhausted and exhilarated. The old adage, *you never know what you can do till you try* is true.

Did you know that only 10 percent of us will take a risk and fulfill our lifetime goals and dreams? Remember the study of those ninety-five-year-olds? At a point in their lives when it's almost too late, they regretted not seeing more, doing more, and taking more risks.

After you've laughed over my trials and tribulations, which ended on a positive note, I hope you won't wait until it's almost too late to take a few risks and turn *your own* goals and dreams into reality.

Now it's all about you. . . .

Are you are ready to take back *your* power? Most likely your #1 concern is to make enough money to cover your bills, pay for some life coaching, or business training, and some sharp-looking new clothes.

Maybe your makeover includes a career change, starting your own business, or returning to work after raising your children. Here are some risk-taking tips that I wish I'd known before I left the White Cliffs of Dover.

Your initial job search can leave you standing on shaky ground. Like me, you may discover that what was expected of you *in the past* is a mere shadow of what is expected of you *now*. After a couple of stressful interviews, the stakes get higher. You may feel shocked as you are asked, like a bolt out of the blue, "You are fluent in French aren't you?" Or, "You are an expert with Excel spread sheets, aren't you?" Or, "You can make crêpes Suzette, can't you?"

You may not get hired or close the deal that day because someone else had those special skills. Just when you thought you had the job in *your* pocket, you had a sinking feeling that your pocket had a hole in it. . .

The latest gloomy statistics reveal that the U.S. job market will slowly return to its pre-recession figures between the close of 2015 and 2021.* By the time *your* local job market picks up it may be too late for you to save your home, your marriage, and your sanity!

How would you feel if you could turn the tide in your favor?

Richard Koch, in his study of the 80/20 principle, tells us that only 20 percent of us will become winners, while 80 percent will not.*

Sales competition is fierce, and the job market is overpopulated, so how can *you* sway the interview to your advantage? In my experience, acquiring the winner's edge is *much* more subtle than you might expect.

So . . . instead of losing out, why not follow these well-kept secrets to becoming a winner at "Hello?"

RISKS AND REWARDS
HOW TO BECOME A WINNER AT "HELLO!"

#1 Do you love me or hate me?
There's a strange phenomenon that often happens when we meet someone new. *For no rational reason, we*

simply hate their guts. This happens right before we shake hands and a single word is spoken.

This strange phenomenon also occurs in sales presentations and job interviews. Do your best to avoid raising the hackles on anyone's back, or giving them any reason to hate you, before you speak. It's like Ripley's "Believe It or Not"! If you've jarred their senses *before* you shake hands, you've lost the job, or the sale at "Hello."

Instead of this illogical disconnect, why not turn it to your advantage by building a rock solid rapport? This is equally as important as having great sales skills, or excellent qualifications for the job.

The best way to build rapport is to let other people do most of the talking while you demonstrate with your body language that you are listening *intently*.

Look them directly in the eye and lean forward slightly in your chair as they speak. If they have an erect posture, sit or stand straight and tall to match their body language. If they are more laid back and relaxed, after a couple of minutes you can allow your body to relax *a little*.

Sounds simple? Trust me, it takes lots of practice. But once you have these rapport skills down pat, people will feel at ease around you, and you'll be perceived as a winner shortly after your first "Hello."

You don't have to have your feet held to the fire, like me. You can learn from my mistakes. If I'd taken a class in rapport skills before I moved to Switzerland, I would have handled my interview with Herr Schneider quite differently. Chances are, with better verbal and non-verbal communication skills, I would have avoided his *do it or be fired* ultimatum.

While we all communicate, few of us connect well enough to get what we want in life.*

#2 Break rapport and you may still lose

Congratulations! You've built a solid-gold rapport with your VIP customer, or your brand new boss. Now you must maintain it. Maintaining rapport means you must be more *interested* than *interesting*.

Again, please learn from my mistakes . . . .

Years ago, at the beginning of my risk-taking adventures and brand new to rapport building, I lost a fabulous training job with an international company sixty minutes after my first "Hello."

On a hot and sticky Tuesday in London, I found myself in an equally sticky situation with a local department head. While I'd been told the job was a slam dunk, I wanted insights into the company's problems so I could personalize my presentation. Before we talked business, my first priority was to establish a rock-solid rapport. This meant listening patiently and intently while she complained nonstop about the day-to-day challenges of her job.

"I know *you* love working overseas, but I hate it," she wailed. "I'm completely exhausted! I just came back from this *terrible* trade show in Brazil. I was utterly miserable for four weeks. It was hot and dirty, I hated the food, and the people were rude and hostile. As if *that* wasn't bad enough, I don't speak a word of Spanish."

"But they speak *Portuguese* in Brazil," I gasped.

Her face turned bright red, and she stormed out, slamming the door behind her. My contract was like one of those *Mission Impossible* assignments: It self-destructed sixty seconds later.

"But the words just slipped out," I muttered, attempting to justify my actions.

Once you've built a good rapport, *no words should just slip out*. Your role is to be more interested than interesting. You are not there to outsmart your customer or interviewer; you are there to create a connection that will stand the test of time. Just because you have an educational edge on them doesn't mean you should flaunt it!

#3 Ten seconds and you win or lose

You have only ten seconds to make a good first impression, and over 50 percent of that first impression is based on your posture and appearance. Believe it or not, this is good news.

The way you present yourself is one thing that is *completely* under your control. Your posture as you walk in the door will make either a good first impression or a bad one. Walk confidently, with your shoulders back and head erect, even if, deep down, you are *desperate* to get hired or sign a deal that day.

Here's more good news: Acting *as if* you are confident, even when you are not, gradually shifts your testosterone levels to match those of someone who is naturally self-assured. Yes, testosterone is a sex hormone, so if this leads to more hanky-panky in your sex life, isn't this is a win-win situation?

#4 Power up with your professional dress.

If you are old enough to dress yourself, you are old enough to know that some looks are déclassé in a professional setting. Two inches of cleavage can look fabulous at a bodacious party in Manhattan, but it doesn't work in the boardroom, unless you work in the porn industry!

Two inches of underwear showing above your pants is never appropriate in a business setting, even if you *are* the Olympic snowboarding champion.

Pierced ears are fine, but if you have any other body parts pierced, think twice before you flash these appendages at your interviewer. I guarantee they will *Flashdance* you out of there the moment you say "Hello."

Please wear business clothes to business interviews, in *credibility* colors: navy blue, light blue, black, beige, grey, and white. Not your favorite colors? Just *grin and wear it* if you want to look like a winner.

#5 Winning self-confidence skills.

Fear is a critical factor in important meetings, job interviews, and sales presentations. I can't count the number of times I've wanted to use my favorite FEAR strategy: Forget Everything And Run.

"What would a winner do?" asks J.B. Gossinger, the Morning Coach.*

Here are three winning strategies that always worked for me:

- Get up and sing to some cheerful music
- Dress up
- Act up. Act like a winner even if you don't feel like it.

Dressing up is a significant part of being a winner. People treat you better when you are well dressed. Even if you are going to the grocery store, or the gym, wear a jaunty cap, or a colorful scarf. Developing your own sense of style is one of the best confidence boosters on the planet. **

If you have panic attacks and/or social anxiety it's tough to act like a winner. I recommend three Bach flower essences: Mimulus for fear, Aspen for panic attacks, and Larch for self-confidence. They can help you stay cool, calm, and collected at gut-wrenching social events and grueling job interviews.

#6 Taking the next big step

If you were hired or closed the deal in another state or country, it's like being married by proxy; you don't really know what you're getting yourself into. Like a bride in an arranged marriage meeting her ninety-year-old bridegroom at the altar, you may be in for a big shock!

First of all, *it's not your fault.* Please understand that what your on-site boss/big-shot client considers critical may seem inconsequential to the local buyer/interviewer thousands of miles away. Watch, listen, and learn exactly what is expected from you. This might include learning a new skill set or even a whole new language!

Instead of feeling overwhelmed by the tasks ahead, focus on developing three skills that set you apart as a top notch winner: risk-taking, rapport building, and resilience.**

Now thank your lucky stars that you are familiar with taking risks and dealing with daily challenges. Risk-taking increases your self-confidence at lightning speed and catapults you light years ahead of the competition.

#7 Every leap of faith takes fell swooping

Here's the most important lesson I learned from leaping out of my comfort zone into the unknown. We can't re-create ourselves in one fell swoop. It takes lots of fell swooping, or should I say *fowl* swooping?

Risk-taking turns us into golden eagles. We swoop down to gather some courage and self-confidence one day, and then swoop down to get insights and inspiration the next.

While we'll quickly achieve some successes in those first fell swoops, it can take months of swooping and soaring to turn our long-term goals into reality. Yes, I was offered a good job in a gorgeous location, yet I had to swoop and soar for months to *keep* it.

How did I stay the course and how did I cope? This book holds all the secrets.

After a year of feasting on fattening prosciutto and creamy pasta fungoli, my waistline had widened from extra small to extra large. Even worse, the stress of my demanding job *and* my difficult divorce was making my hair fall out in handfuls. I eliminated several stress-inducing foods from my diet and quickly lost fifteen pounds while my hair grew back thicker than ever. *See Chapter 8.*

I discovered the Mushroom/Toadstool principle – insightful ways to determine those people I could trust and those I should avoid like the plague. For risk-takers, our future livelihoods – and even our lives – depend on us being able to tell the difference. *See Chapter 4.*

Most of us get so fired up while we are re-inventing ourselves that we may overlook our mates. It's not a win-win situation to have a hot new career or renewed sense of purpose and an ice-cold, indignant love partner. Have you wondered why many Oscar and Grammy winners go through a separation in the same year? Why not reignite your love relationship while you are reinventing the rest of your life? *See Chapter 9.*

It's my belief that depression, anxiety, and fatigue, so prevalent in our world today, are caused by suppressed creativity. Once we unleash our creative potential, our lives become passionate and purposeful – powerful beyond measure. Do *you* want to experience a creative miracle? Then don't miss *Chapter 7.*

Try these simple risks for yourself, and here's what you'll see. The next time you walk into a room crowded with your colleagues or competitors, nobody will shout, "O hell! O no!" as they head out the door.

Rather they will say, "Hellooo" (four syllables). "I've heard so many great things about you. Would you be interested in working for my company? We need someone with your top-notch communication skills."

Congratulations, you hit the jackpot! You've become a winner at "Hello."

* See References and Research

** See How to Beat Monday Morning Blues p.202

CHAPTER 3

WINNING OVER YOUR GREATEST FEARS

YOU CAN BE SCARED OR SUCCESSFUL— WHICH ONE WILL YOU CHOOSE?

"Leap and the net will appear." —Julia Cameron

"Jump, señora, Dios mío, salte!"

"I *can't* do it. I'm terrified of heights," I screamed back.

It was a hot and sultry day in the Costa Rican rainforest. A pungent smell of bark and berries permeated the air after pounding rain and bolts of lightning had lashed the palm trees, bending their branches to the ground.

I was standing on a slippery wooden platform 100 feet in the air. In five short minutes my mood had gone from anxious and fearful to panic-stricken and petrified.

It had taken every ounce of my courage to climb the slithery, moss- covered steps to the top. Now I was staring over the treetops at the brackish river below and muttering, "No, no, I've changed my mind. I just can't do it. I'm turning back."

But to my dismay, it seemed that turning back was not an option. . . .

"No way back, *señora*. You must jump," said Alfredo, my leathery-skinned guide.

Fear was stabbing in my throat as if I'd swallowed a prickly aloe plant. I glanced behind me, only to see the steps I had climbed alone in the storm were now packed with eager beaver jumpers of all shapes and sizes who seemed most anxious to meet their maker.

"Is this why it's called the death slide? You do it and then die from the combination of shock, stress and sheer terror?" I screamed.

One hour earlier, as we drove through the gates to this beautiful rainforest preserve, I'd been handed a ticket.

"Free ticket to the death slide today," Alfredo explained. "It's free because we had sooo many storms. Most of our tourists are afraid to jump in the rain."

"Afraid they might die, on the death slide?" I asked. "Surely the name gives you a big clue?"

Once again the heavens opened, and sheets of rain drenched my thin cotton T-shirt and shorts. I was shivering from the combination of being soaking wet and scared to death.

"Go, go, *señora*. I follow right behind you. You jump now, OK."

In a tropical downpour, I leapt from the wobbly wooden platform, barely wide enough for two people, and whizzed over the treetops on a thin metal wire. Alfredo euphemistically called this insane activity zip-lining, but I called it. . . something else!

These were some of the scariest moments of my life. My teeth were chattering and my legs were trembling as I zipped over the gushing, muddy-brown river 100 feet below me.

Astonished buzzards with six-foot wingspans flew alongside me wondering, *What the heck is this human being doing – trying to fly like a bird?*

"I was wondering the same thing," I told them, but apparently I don't speak buzzard!

"Please, God, let me land safely at the other side," I sobbed. "Don't let me be headline news in tomorrow's paper." *British author bites the dust on the death slide. Her latest book on risk-taking will be published posthumously.*

There's nothing like facing one's imminent death to get one to pray fervently. As I whizzed down the slippery wire in the storm, I prayed as if these were my last moments on earth. Sure enough, my prayers were answered and I was plummeted slap-bang into the arms of an angel. Not the arms of a winged angel waiting at the pearly gates, but the arms of a gorgeous, muscular Costa Rican.

"So I *did* die and go to heaven?" I muttered as I slowly opened one eye.

"No, *señora*, I save you. Now I take you to the next slide," he replied.

"What do you mean *next* slide? I'm done here."

"No, *señora*, this is the first slide in a series of seven."

"So, if the first one doesn't get you, the sixth or seventh one will," I mumbled.

How many times have you taken a giant leap of faith only to discover that you weren't done? You had at least six more gigantic leaps of faith ahead of you.

Are you are serious about transforming yourself and having a life filled with happiness and success? Facing your fears is paramount if you want to be a winner in your personal and professional lives!

I'm not suggesting you build a zip-line in your back yard, or be a contestant on *Survivor* and slash your way through dense undergrowth in the rainforest. But the risk I'm asking you to take today may feel just as gut wrenching. It's called *public speaking*.*

"No, no, don't ask me to do *that*," you are probably saying.

Just like slithering down the death slide, your heart may be pounding and your knees knocking as you wrap your mind around this risk.

"But I'd just open my mouth and nothing would come out," most people say.

"While public speaking is the world's number one fear, it's like eating an elephant: you tackle it one bite at a time," I reassure them.*

It's OK. I won't ask you to address a packed audience in London's Albert Hall; but I will ask you to take a few risks to improve your communication skills. That means saying *Yes* rather than *No* to some things that will scare the bejeebers out of you.

And to prove my point, here's my very first, and I hope my very last, embarrassing moment on another kind of platform.

New to risk-taking *and* public speaking, I'd spent five years working in Switzerland, France, and Denmark. In these cultured epicurean countries, the only outrageous risks I'd taken were the daily assaults on my *digestion*.

I was brought up on a bland British diet of Shepherd's Pie and rice pudding. Now my stomach was in shock as it fought to digest pickled herring and pâté de foie gras, washed down with copious amounts of Cabernet, Perrier, and Dom Pérignon.

Out of the blue I was offered a job in Central America. For me this was treacherous risk-taking territory.

I spent a year coaching a celebrity author, whose willpower had crumbled during a contentious divorce and she'd gained fifty pounds. I coached her to lose a significant amount of weight, adopt a healthy lifestyle, and write some of her best chapters. When my contract was up, I took six weeks off to explore the rainforest and practice my poor Spanish on the unsuspecting locals.

Facing my fear of heights in a tropical downpour had unleashed an astonishing outcome. Once I'd landed unscathed after seven death slides, I felt indomitable. I could do *anything*.

If you feel invincible as you step on that platform, please learn from *my* mistakes. If you act like an egotistical King Kong and believe that nothing can go wrong, get ready for a giant-sized downfall.

It was a sweltering summer's day in San José, Costa Rica. I was prepped and ready to give my first international speech in English to a prestigious bilingual audience.

After leaping into the abyss seven times in a row, my head had grown seven sizes bigger. Much to my shame and chagrin, I felt quixotically confident that I could make some casual opening remarks in Spanish.

What I attempted to say was, "I am embarrassed because my Spanish is so weak."

Translated, what I actually said was, *"I am weak because I am so pregnant."* Embarazada is Spanish for expecting or pregnant!

When Shakespeare wrote about the *pregnant pause* in *A Midsummer Night's Dream*, even his creative mind could not have conceived this communication faux pas. My words were met with a dramatic response. The audience's initial stunned reaction was followed by a loud gasp of shock.

Try regaining control of a posh international crowd when you have just announced to all and sundry that you feel weak because you are *sooo pregnant.*

Forget about my well-crafted humorous speech – I had set a darker stage, and I was now playing the lead role in a horror movie of my own making.

The video camera that was trained on me immediately swung over to Fernando, the executive director who had hired me for this event. Without any doubt, in my audience's minds, Fernando was the father of my unborn child.

This handsome Antonio de Banderas look-alike now turned beet red with embarrassment. No matter how much I tried to apologize for my wretched Spanish, it was already too late – *the damage had been done.*

Costa Rica is a devoutly Catholic country, and my well-heeled audience had been handed a burning mission - to save both me *and* my unborn baby. There was an atmospheric shift in the room that would have melted a polar ice cap.

The mixture of tension and excitement in the air was escalating like a fire blazing in the rain forest. I glanced around and noticed – shock/horror – that nobody was looking me in the eye. All eyes were focused on my *stomach,* to see if it was protruding anywhere!

How did I survive this sword-swallowing humiliation? I had two things going for me. I was well rehearsed, and I'd recently become an expert in facing code red, fearsome situations. So I made it through the rest of my speech without frothing at the mouth or falling down in a dead faint. I didn't look back, but I'm sure I left a big puddle of sweat behind on the stage.

As I exited the auditorium, the men in the audience were slapping the (allegedly) expectant father on the back and congratulating him.

"Fernando, you devil, you! When's the wedding?"

I glanced at Fernando, and he gave me the mafia slit-throat signal, which left me in no doubt that our friendship was over, forever!

Meanwhile, the women in the audience were more sympathetic. Crowding protectively round me they asked. . .

"When is the baby due?"
"Is this your first child? Don't worry, I have five children."
"Fernando, he's a good man. He'll make a good father."

I shook hands with the CEO. "I've added a little extra to your check for the *baby*," he whispered. I could tell from the tightness of his grip and the agitated look in his eyes that he was hesitant to let me leave the country before he'd seen me married and made a morally-sound woman!

"You look tired," he said.

"Tired, you're right, I *am* tired," I replied. I was tired of making such a fool of myself.

"Yes, yes, you must go home and rest now," he said, squeezing my hand as a gesture of comfort.

I ran to my rental car and drove like a bat out of hell to the airport.

On a serene British Airways flight back to Heathrow, I mused over my Spanish faux pas. If I'd been this reckless in the rain forest, I'd have ended up dead. In the speaking world, I'd shot myself in the foot, and I was limping contritely back to London.

There's no way to sugarcoat the reality that public speaking comes with its own set of risks. No matter how perfect your presentation, or how skilled you have become as a speaker, sometimes things *will* go wrong.

Thank your lucky stars that daily risk-taking has taught you to stay cool, calm, and collected when the roof caves in, the A/V equipment fails, or your audience is too inebriated to care after drinking too many cherry-topped cocktails.

Just relax and pay attention to your gut reaction. You will be given distinct warning signals when things are about to go wrong . . . *dead wrong!*

It was high noon on a hot and muggy day in Honolulu, Hawaii. The temperature was soaring, the sun was sweltering, and I felt as if I had stepped onto the set of the TV show *Hawaii Five-0*.

I was in a prestigious beachfront hotel surrounded by paparazzi, with their dark glasses, diamond earrings, and bling overkill. Bling was gleaming from their belt buckles, their rhinestone sun glasses, and their supersized sequined tote bags.

I immediately renamed them the *glitterati paparazzi*.

While the wind was rustling through the palm trees outside the hotel, inside the paparazzi were rustling through their programs, as high-speed TV cameras whirred softly in the background.

"Who is she," I heard in Japanese, French, and English. *"What's she going to talk about?"*

That "she" was ME.

My keynote topic – how to write and self-publish a book – would be given to this illustrious audience of journalists and newscasters. For some unknown reason, my legs were shaking, and I felt queasy in the pit of my stomach.

This was not a sudden attack of pre-speech nerves. Surprisingly, I'd *woken up* feeling this way. It was nothing I could put my finger on. I was well prepared, I had printed directions to the hotel, and a big stack of books to sign, but a little voice in my head kept telling me, *take an extra copy of your introduction with you, just in case.*

"Just in case of *what?*" I asked the voice in my head, and then glanced around to see if anyone had heard me talking to myself.

"OK, OK, I'll do it, *just in case,*" I capitulated.

I printed out a second copy and stapled it to my speech notes. After years of risk-taking, I've learned my lesson. If I ignored that intuitive voice in my head, I'd always live to regret it.

Lunch was being served, and I glanced through my notes while a white-haired journalist, prepped and ready to announce me, stepped up to the microphone with a copy of my introduction in his hand.

"I must have been crazy," I said, berating myself. "I didn't need that extra copy after all. I put myself through an insane amount of stress for *no apparent reason.*"

My elegant introducer adjusted his rhinestone reading glasses and announced, "Our keynote speaker today is Suzanne St. George." A split second after he spoke my name, he crumpled to the floor in a dead faint.

Let's be honest here - I've always dreamed of having a mesmerizing effect on my audiences. I've always hoped they would say, "You were such a fantastic storyteller, I was in a trance." It never, ever, crossed my mind that someone might pass out at the mere mention of my name.

The head paparazzo immediately phoned for the paramedics and then motioned for me to step up to the podium.

But I was glued to my chair. I couldn't move. "This can't be happening!" I said out loud.

"Get on up here, Suzanne," he snapped impatiently as he stepped over the motionless body. "I've dialed 911, so just leave him on the floor and go ahead and *introduce yourself.*"

"You've got to be kidding. I *can't* step on that stage – there's a *body behind the podium*," I attempted to say. But when I opened my mouth, nothing came out.

My feet felt as if they were in blocks of clay as I surveyed the scene before me. The past few minutes had felt completely surreal, as if I were on the set of a science fiction movie.

"Any minute now, I will wake up and this will all have been a bad dream," I muttered. But no, this was real! Whether I liked it or not, I was "on."

Agatha Christie and Stephen King would know what to do here, but I did not. I reached over his limp body to grab the microphone and turned back to face the audience. Of course, I couldn't *use* the podium to prop up my notes, as it was completely blocked by his sprawling legs and feet.

I glanced around the room. Everyone appeared laid-back and relaxed – except *me*. Then it hit me, like a bolt of lightning. Paparazzi take photos of lifeless bodies every day, so this was nothing new or unusual for them. But attempting to speak with a body behind the podium was both new and *terrifying* for me.

Surely it can't get any more nerve-wracking than this, I thought, but it *could. . . .*

After I read my own introduction and was getting into the *body* of my presentation (excuse the pun), the paramedics arrived. Not softly and gently, but with a loud crash bang, they burst through the beautiful stained glass swing doors.

Exactly like in a scene from *Hawaii Five-0*, these movie star look-alikes had spiky hair cuts, six-pack abs, and dazzling toothpaste smiles. The TV cameras immediately swung to capture their faces rather than mine. Just to add to the excitement, they hauled in a bright orange defibrillator and five types of lifesaving devices.

While I love watching *Hawaii Five-0*, I'm used to viewing this high speed drama on the TV, not in the middle of my speech.

Bravely, I plodded on with my story, while a wild commotion continued behind me. Just as I was ready to deliver my punch line, the paramedics shouted "Step aside, ma'am," as they pushed their pale and shaken patient toward the waiting ambulance.

"Does anyone have any questions," I asked in a hoarse voice, as I wondered, *how do I follow that*?

I was expecting my audience to ask, "Is he going to be OK?"

But this was a room full of 007s: they were neither shaken nor stirred. These media warriors had seen it *all*, and they stayed cool, calm, and collected throughout all the chaos and confusion.

Unlike me! This macabre turn of events had left my head spinning and my hands shaking. Here's the good news - *nobody knew it but me.* My years of risk-taking helped me appear relaxed and stress-free despite these unprecedented circumstances.

It was high time to reengage my audience and add some humorous interaction, to counteract all the wild distractions in the room.

"Is anybody else feeling bothered by the heat?" I asked.

"Would you please take your pulse, and say to the person next to you, I'm OK, are you OK?" There was a loud buzz in the room as, much to my surprise, everybody complied.

"I know it's a sweltering ninety degrees out there, but if anyone else is feeling a little faint, I'd like to be forewarned. Don't worry; I'm quite familiar with treating heat stroke.

"Did you know the Queen's Guards at Buckingham Palace drop like flies whenever the temperature soars over eighty degrees? If you've visited the city of London, you'll know this only happens six times a year."

Like all paparazzi they loved stories about the British royals. "Have you met the queen?" a newscaster asked.

"Twice," I replied. "Even better, I visited 10 Downing Street on official business."

I grabbed my audience's attention and held it as I recalled my risk-taking adventures at Number Ten.

What can we learn from these stories? In this exciting new life we are creating, we have to be ready for *any eventuality* – whether it's slithering down a wire strung between the palm trees, embarrassing ourselves by saying inappropriate words, or attempting to deliver a speech during sheer pandemonium.

The following seven tools will serve you well, whether you are speaking to an audience of five hundred at a convention or five associates in a business meeting.

RISKS AND REWARDS
FOR PUBLIC SPEAKING FEARS

#1 Clear the air with a secret weapon.
Once you are ready to give your speech, arrive early and spray the room with Rescue Remedy.* It will calm you, as well as your audience, while giving you a secret advantage.

Never underestimate the importance of arriving early, because you *never* know what you will find. Sometimes your feet will be held to the fire, and you will have to perform emergency damage control.

Three years ago I was a speaker at a conference breakout session at a four-star beachfront hotel in

Florida. I arrived one hour early to find the room I'd been allocated was occupied by a gentlemen's luncheon club.

These "gentlemen" were beyond drunk and disorderly; not one of them could string a complete sentence together. Instead they were screaming, shouting, and tossing bread sticks at one another. It was a total uproar, and not only that; it was a *speaker's nightmare*. They'd drunk far too much vino and were having far too much fun to vacate the room for me.

Despite a dozen anguished phone calls to the hotel manager, he was nowhere to be found. Meanwhile my audience was gathering on the mezzanine. Many of them had that *deer in the headlights* look, wondering whether they should stick around to see what happened or make a mad dash for safety.

I had to take a risk, along with some immediate action – or lose my entire audience, along with my paycheck. I climbed on a chair, banged a large metal tray, and made an impassioned plea for the revelers to move their unruly butts to the tiki bar. I tipped the waiters lavishly to clear the room, while I bonded with my audience in the hallway.

Once the room was cleaned up, I sprayed the air with Rescue Remedy before swallowing the rest of the bottle to steady my *own* nerves.

"It's a natural stress reliever," I told one elderly lady who asked what I was doing.

But there was no need for alarm. I explained the benefits of Rescue Remedy in stressful situations, while my audience remained soothed and relaxed and even wrote me wonderful reviews.

Two hours later, I joined the gentlemen revelers at the tiki bar for a glass of red wine and some much-needed R & R.

#2 Win or lose before you say a word?

Win over your audience by shaking hands with everyone before you speak. Clasp their hands firmly and look them directly in the eye as you say, "Thanks for being here today."

The conclusion of your presentation is just as critical. Be willing to stay behind for an additional thirty minutes to answer any sensitive questions off stage. This demonstrates that you are interested in your audience's personal and professional challenges and, most importantly, that you genuinely care.

#3 What if your heart is in your boots?

If you allow fear and anxiety to surge through your body, it virtually guarantees things will go badly. You can shift your attitude by shifting your posture.

Practice using a powerful posture and stance. Take up more space by using big gestures and moving around the platform with a sense of purpose. Despite how you feel *inside*, when you move purposefully you will create a compelling onstage presence.

Acting as if you feel self-confident – even when you feel scared to death – decreases the stress hormone cortisol while it increases your sex hormones! Have you noticed how many captivating speakers have a special charisma? It all boils down to the amount of passion hormones they have pulsating through their veins.

#4 I'll get up there and forget everything.

Memorize the opening and closing lines of your presentation. This will help manage your fears. Write a few memory joggers on the inside of a manila folder with a marker pen. Keep the folder closed until you reach the podium. It's essential to be so familiar with your material that you can speak comfortably from a one- or two-word prompt.

Yes, that means . . . . practice, practice, practice.*

#5 Grab their attention in 60 seconds.

If you don't, you're toast!

Have a powerful opening line and follow this up with an interesting story. No, I don't recommend you announce to all and sundry that you are weak and pregnant – unless you are selling a product to alleviate morning sickness!

If you are speaking to make a sale, the same rules apply. Most sales professionals experience resistance that can ruin their presentation. On the other hand, few of us can resist a good story told eloquently. Your best solution is to perfect your story-telling skills. This will bring both your story, and your sale, to a successful conclusion.**

#6 Should I be funny?

If you are a brand-new speaker, I recommend steering clear of any and all jokes. Being funny onstage takes nerves of steel and eons of practice. While I'm an entertaining, humorous, speaker, I spent years taking acting classes before I could pull off onstage humor successfully.

If you decide to tell a joke, please poke fun at *yourself*, not someone in the company, or a TV personality. I guarantee this type of sarcastic humor will offend more people than it will entertain.

#7 Speaking? Still scared or successful?

If you are nervously shaking your head and saying, "No, no, I couldn't do *that*; I'm much too scared," let me say this. . . .

Speaking out, whether it's to a small group of people or a larger professional audience, is the fastest way to build your self-confidence. I guarantee you will have some tongue-tied moments that will leave you quaking in your boots. Even though the outcome can be acutely embarrassing, it's not life threatening!

Once you conquer your fear of public speaking you will be the most successful salesperson on your team and/or the most sought-after date on the singles scene. Yes, it requires taking a few risks, but so does landing that million-dollar sale, or going on a first date with that good-looking guy or gal.

Now you are left with only two choices . . . . You can be scared or successful. Which one will *you* choose?

* See References and Research
** See Courage and Adventure Skills for Women, p.201

CHAPTER 4

WHO CAN YOU TRUST, AND WHO SHOULD YOU AVOID LIKE THE PLAGUE?

THE SECRET LIES IN THEIR SIGNATURE!

"If not now, When?" —The Talmud

It was ten o'clock on a steamy Sunday morning in East Africa, and I had to pinch myself to make sure I wasn't dreaming. I was standing within shouting distance of the equator, preparing to embark on a gigantic adventure. Even at this hour, the sunbaked ground was so unbearably hot that it burned my feet through my soft safari sandals.

But this was not a typical Sunday; this was about to become one of the scariest Sundays of my entire life. . .

I was prepped and ready for a seven-day photographic safari that would take me to some remote parts of a lion preserve. While I'd been working in Nairobi, Kenya for the past six months I was still a *Lonely Planet* type of traveler. I'd always take the unconventional, adventurous path rather than a guided tour. On this day, that adventurous path nearly turned into a *deadly* path . . .

"Here, hold my flight log while I grab another cup of coffee," said a good-looking man fighting off what appeared to be a gigantic hangover. "I had far too many gin fizzes last night."

While his hangover was no immediate cause for concern, the fact that he was wearing a crumpled shirt that said *safari pilot* on it *was*.

"Oh no, don't tell me this is *my* safari pilot," I said, not really wanting to know the answer.

I glanced down at his scrawled handwriting and signature and *my blood ran cold*. Should I run for cover, or fake a sudden illness, so I could avoid what appeared to be my imminent demise?

"Wait a minute, maybe I was wrong," I said out loud. "Take a deep breath Suzanne; calm yourself down before you look again."

No, No, I was right the first time.

What his blotchy, erratic handwriting revealed was that this man was either an axe murderer or an out-of-control alcoholic with zero clarity of judgment. Neither of these was an admirable attribute for someone who would be piloting me, in a single-engine plane, across the dangerous Rift Valley to the border of Kenya and Tanzania.*

Six weeks earlier I had taken a weekend course in handwriting analysis. Did I have enough information to make such life and death decisions? I wondered. After all, we *all* have bad days when we stay up too late, eat too many deserts, or drink too many cocktails with a cherry on top.

And, after all, I was a *risk taker*.

"We're missing two passengers?" he asked. "Where the dickens are they? We've got to take off ASAP to stay ahead of this storm. O jolly good, here they come. Do you speak German?"

His words were rolled into one high-speed sentence that sounded more like gibberish than English, and his hands were visibly shaking as he checked us off the passenger list.

"O lawdy, maybe he's just as high as a kite from the Kenyan coffee jitters," I muttered.

The German tourists smiled and waved as they hurried across the rustic-looking terminal building with its rough-hewn roof and red stone floor. I felt as if I were on the set of *Out of Africa*. The wind was picking up outside, whipping through the palm fronds and bending tall, yellow grasses to the ground.

As our remaining two passengers approached, their smiles turned to troubled looks. They stared anxiously at our hung-over pilot and whispered together.

"Alrighty folks, it's time to get airborne. There's bad weather heading our way, so let's get cracking."

"Did he say cracking, as in crack–ing?" I muttered. "Maybe his weird handwriting means he's on *crack cocaine*."

It was too late to fake a sudden illness. Our pilot, high on caffeine and heaven knows what else, was marching us out of the dilapidated terminal and toward our plane.

"Surely that *can't* be our plane," I said as I stared at this battered flying machine that looked as if it should be hanging from the roof of the Smithsonian, rather than sitting on the runway, ready to take off.

The movie playing out before me was shifting from the elegant *Out of Africa* to the Kenyan version of *Pirates of the Caribbean*. In the dazzling sunlight, it was hard to miss that our bad-boy pilot was a dead ringer for Johnny Depp. All he needed was an eye patch and an earring and *caramba*, they could have been twins.

Wait a minute; didn't Johnny Depp make his prisoners walk the plank? Instead of walking it, we were scrambling aboard our very own flying plank . . . .
Will I reach my campsite, or will I disappear over the Rift Valley, never to be seen again? I wondered miserably.

I was about to find out. . . .

"Pride comes before a fall," my mother had declared six weeks earlier, when I proclaimed that I could determine a mushroom - someone you can trust –

from a toadstool - someone you should avoid like the plague – by analyzing their handwriting.

Could she be right? Was I about to encounter a hideous downfall for presuming that in forty-eight hours, I could become a professional handwriting expert?

I turned to my fellow passengers in an attempt to allay my panic.

"*Hallo. Ich heisse Suzanne. Wie ghets*?" I asked, hoping that my voice wouldn't tremble with fear and trepidation.

"*Gut, gut*," they answered, but from the frightened looks on their faces, it seemed that they were just as terrified as me.

After a couple of hours of wild rolling and pitching over the Rift Valley, I was ready to scream, "Hand me a parachute or put this plane down on the ground right *now!*" But as I started to speak, I was interrupted.

"Hold on tight, folks! I've got to make a sharp turn," our rambunctious bush pilot yelled, like Johnny Depp would say as he swung his pirate schooner around. "I overshot the runway with these crosswinds. So I've got to take another stab at it."

"Are we there *already*?" I asked, trying to hide the obvious relief in my voice.

"*They* are," he replied, pointing to the German couple. "You've still got a long way to go till we reach the border."

The Germans shot me a sympathetic look as they scrambled out of the plane and into a waiting jeep that whisked them away to their safe safari lodge.

Before I had time to catch my breath and conjure up some excuse to remain on the ground, he'd revved up the engine, and once again we were off and rolling down the runway!

"What's the name of your safari campsite again?" he asked irritably as we leveled off.

"But. . . I gave you all my paperwork at the airport," I stammered.

"Well it's *not here*," he said, waving his clipboard at me. His face was now bright red and contorted with rage. "Besides, I need the *exact* coordinates, not just some flimsy pieces of paper."

This was not an appropriate time to point out to a potential axe murderer/alcoholic that coordinates were usually something you determined *before* you took off, not while you were in the air.

I grabbed his clipboard and searched for my paperwork, but now it was *my* timing that was off. As I leaned forward, the plane took a sharp nosedive into an air pocket, and I felt sick in the pit of my stomach.

It was certainly not the right time to distract my cantankerous pilot. I needed him to focus all his remaining brain cells on keeping us airborne.

It was too late. He was already distracted. . . .

During our nosedive I had grabbed his arm along with the instrument panel to steady myself.

"So, sweetie, you want to *fool around*?" he asked, squeezing my thigh and grinning broadly.

"O lawdy, I wasn't prepared for *this*," I mumbled. Who knew I would be spending my Sunday flying over the Rift Valley with a hung-over pilot who was in search of a sex-starved playmate?

"Maybe we should return to the safari lodge till we can figure this out?" I suggested, trying to keep my voice cool, calm, and somewhat collected as I removed his hand from my thigh.

I said *we* because, while I can read nautical charts, I had no idea how to read aeronautical charts. Besides, if I wanted to stay alive, throwing a fit or casting blame could bring this day to a calamitous end.

Maddened by my rejection, his mood went from bad to worse.

"No, no. It's too late to turn back. I'll radio Governor's Camp and tell them that I'm dropping you off. It's close by, and I don't have enough fuel to go wandering around the sky, searching for some mystery campsite," he snapped. "Besides, I'm *sure* that's where you are supposed to be."

Phew! At least he had a clear destination in mind, and soon I would be safe and sound, on the ground.

He switched on the radio, and I heard a loud crackling noise that reminded me of an old Hitchcock movie. He left a brief message about dropping a passenger off on the airstrip and hung up.

I hoped this was one of those rare Hitchcock movies that had a happy ending. . . .

Twenty minutes later, I was on the ground, but I was *not* safe, and I was *not* at the right destination.

"Where's the campsite?" I asked nervously.

"It's over there, somewhere," he said, sweeping his suntanned arm in a wide 180-degree curve.

"But nobody's here to meet me."

"Don't worry, *after* I take off I will radio them again and let them know you are waiting on the airstrip.
They probably didn't respond earlier because they're battening down the hatches preparing for this storm."

"OK, I've gotta go if I'm going to stay ahead of this front. I'll see you in a few days."

"Don't go. *Please don't go.* Stay with me till somebody gets here," I sobbed.

Without a scrap of concern for my safety, he took off, leaving me all alone on a muddy airstrip in the middle of the jungle.

"I'm so *lonely*! Sometimes I feel I'm the loneliest person on the planet," my single friends will say.

"You don't know the meaning of *lonely* until you are all alone in the middle of the jungle, with no one to protect you and without a pellet gun to fire warning shots over any marauding animals," I tell them.

As for me, I was ill equipped to face this life-threatening situation in the middle of lion country. I had no radio, no hunting rifle, and there wasn't a tree tall enough to hide in, if I was forced to spend the night out there.

The next ninety minutes felt like ninety years. They were the longest and loneliest minutes of my life. I prayed that I wouldn't panic because panic is the deadliest emotion to display in the jungle.

By now it was late afternoon and approaching the time when a local pride of lions would be waking up and wondering, *what's for dinner?* Any moment now, some hungry daddy lion would leave his den to look for a slow-moving, terrified target . . . *and that would be me.*

I heard a loud roar in the distance as if some ravenous pride had picked up on my petrified thoughts. Wooa, it was time to fall to my knees and pray to be found while it was still daylight and before the male lions began their nightly prowl.

I swore that if survived this adventure, I would take my handwriting studies more seriously, so that I could make swift and accurate assessments about the writer's character defects.

Finally, my prayers were answered. A cloud of dust appeared on the horizon as a jet-black Masai driver screeched to a halt in his open jeep. I sobbed with relief as he yelled, "Jambo bwana!"

"Jambo" I waved back. "Habari yako."

Even in my distressed state, it was hard to ignore that Mr. Masai looked like an ad for *Muscle* magazine. But, unlike most ads, this man was definitely not airbrushed! His taut, muscular body was barely covered except for some skimpy satin shorts, two sizes too small, and a string of lion-tooth beads.

But wait a minute! I'd barely escaped being mauled by a hungry lion, and a hung-over pilot, only to face another potential pat down! I'd prayed to be saved from the wild animals only to be "saved" by a wild-looking man. But I wasn't about to ask if he would scrawl his signature in the mud before heading off into the jungle.

I tried to ease the tension by explaining, in my poor Swahili, that he was perfectly dressed for a night out in Miami's South Beach, rather than a night in the jungle. But it didn't translate well and he thought I was mad at him.

"Sorry, bwana, I was late. I was on safari with some big shots."

"Big shots, you mean big guns?" I asked nervously.

"No, bwana, big shot hunters from Kenya and Tanzania. We've been searching for a bad ju ju lion. He killed two of our men last month."

My blood, which was boiling a few minutes ago, now ran cold as he recalled the lion killer story in gory detail. I thanked my lucky stars that I was safe and sound in a large Land Rover with two high-powered hunting rifles on the back seat.

As if I hadn't had enough excitement for the day, Mr. Masai took me on a hair-raising, high-speed drive to the elite Governor's Camp.* This campsite is an exclusive meeting place for government ministers and well-heeled adventurers from all over the world.

One hour later at Governor's Camp, I experienced the African version of Ripley's "Believe It or Not." I was reading a wine list that would have delighted most gourmands, and a menu that would rival those of the best restaurants in Paris.

What can you learn from my brush-with-death journey into lion country and ending up in the wrong place at the wrong time?

First, as you embark on an adventure to transform your life, you must have some clear, *written destination* in mind. If you prefer a visual image, why not build an Adventure Board displaying your goals and dreams?* It doesn't matter whether your Adventure Board shows images of a slimmed-down, healthier you, or a happier, more successful you, traveling to exotic destinations.

Second, any time you notice that someone's handwriting is heavy and blotchy, or their signature is erratic, with the letters going in different directions, see this as a red-flag warning. Ask an expert for an opinion ASAP, especially if this "someone" has a hand in your money management or has asked for your hand in marriage.

If you skip these two simple steps, *other people* will control your destiny, and you will end up in a place that is chosen *for* you, rather than a destination you would have chosen.

It doesn't matter if this person is taking you over the Rift Valley or taking you for another kind of ride. Both are equally dangerous to your finances and your future.

"Does this handwriting stuff really work?" people ask me all the time.

I would venture to say that it works so well that in high-profile lawsuits, jurors are often selected by handwriting specialists, or graphologists. Many high-powered legal eagles will pay small fortunes to have the handwriting of their jurors analyzed. Experts can tell how jurors will respond under pressure and how they can be swayed.

Have you ever been stunned when, in an apparently open-and-shut case, the foreman announces a verdict that is the complete antithesis of what was expected? In these cases, I always ask whether a handwriting expert was used in the jury selection. If so, the reason for this volatile verdict may lie in the most unexpected place – right under the judge's nose.

How about you? Would you like to boost your success and self-confidence with the stroke of a pen?

"Yes, yes, tell me how. Tell me now."

For years I've been asked, "Suzanne, can't you just wave a magic wand and transform me overnight?"

"I wish it were that easy!" I reply.

While we all love quick fixes, the reality is that transforming ourselves into someone who is self-confident, compassionate, and capable of handling any challenge, takes time, effort, and determination.

Here's the good news. There's one highly effective, well-kept secret that *works really fast, is easy to follow, and is right at your fingertips.*

Did you know that every time you scribble your signature you are leaving a personality stamp on the page? Your signature reveals your self-confidence and creativity levels, along with your feelings about yourself – both good and bad.

Handwriting is *brain* writing, and to the well-trained eye, your handwriting reveals more than you can possibly imagine about your emotional well-being, or lack of it.

It's astonishing, but true, that when we choose to make small, but focused changes to our signature and handwriting, we can shift our outlook on life from positive to negative.

Most intriguing of all – handwriting will reveal whether the writer is a mushroom – someone you can trust – or a toadstool – someone you should avoid like the plague. This critical insight can protect us from making terrible mistakes *and* can even save our lives.

While handwriting analysis is a well-proven science, please remember that people's moods can change, along with their signatures. While we all have bad hair days, we also have bad signature days, when life throws us a curve. To prove my point, why not study the signatures of past American presidents, hopefully some of the smartest people around. Their signatures are clearly different on *bad* days, when their popularity is down in the polls, as opposed to *good* days, when their ratings are flying high.

Are you ready to become a modern-day Sherlock Holmes? Here are some sleuthing risks to take along with their tantalizing rewards. .

RISKS AND REWARDS
TO INCREASE YOUR SELF-CONFIDENCE

#1 Build credibility with your signature.
Write or sign all your letters with blue ink. Blue ink symbolizes credibility and integrity. Use a blue roller-ball pen, or a fountain pen, rather than a ballpoint. Ballpoint pens can leave blotches that will ruin the credible image you wish to portray.

Toss out your ten-cent Bic that leaks ink all over your fingers and invest in a sharp-looking pen that makes a power statement whenever you sign your name. It doesn't matter whether you are signing a grocery-store check or a million-dollar contract, your pen should make you feel fabulous every time you use it.

#2 Size matters in your signature too!
Size is important and the same rule applies with our signatures. Check the size of your signature; is it small and cramped, or is it larger than the rest of your writing? If your signature is smaller, this can reveal a reserved personality, or shyness in a social setting.

Whether you are searching for a new job or reinventing yourself as a more sociable, self-confident person, start today to write your signature a little larger than usual. Increasing the size of your signature *slightly* indicates that you have a healthy self-image. This can make a huge difference to your social poise and self-assurance and most importantly, how others will perceive you.

Buyer beware! Watch out if you see a signature that is wildly oversized or is written in an outrageous and flamboyant style! An oversized signature signifies that the writer has an oversized opinion of his or her self-importance. This person is conceited, condescending, or "cocky," as we would say in England. If they are selling a flat in Timbuktu, or swampland in Florida, don't be bamboozled into buying.

#3 Angle your signature for more optimism.

Do you want to feel more optimistic? Write your signature, your work notes, and your shopping list on an upward slant. Whenever you write with this upward slant, you are putting an optimistic slant on your feelings.

What if you are struggling with anxiety and depression? Handwriting is brain writing, and if you train your brain to write in this upward, positive and optimistic style, it can shift your outlook on life and its constant challenges.

#4 Strike a pose for self-confidence.

If you would like to present a more confident self-image, then strike a line under your signature. One simple underline, on an upward slant, will give your self-confidence an instant boost.

I know, I know, you are saying, "How can this help? I'm a scaredy cat at cocktail parties and posh social events!"

Take heart and make this your first risk of the day. Even the shyest people I know saw their self-confidence grow in leaps and bounds as they underlined their signatures with a single upward stroke.

Yes, it's faking it till you make it. But most of us start out this way, so you are no different. You are simply choosing to speed up your transformation by using some tried-and-true tools.

Watch out if you see a signature that has several lines scrawled underneath it, creating the image of a pedestal. People who place a pedestal under their signature *believe they belong on one!* This over-the-top, egotistical style only works for rock stars and the already famous.

#5 Natural remedies for self-esteem.

Are you ready to boost your self-esteem? Are you dealing with a myriad of changes in your life, like changing jobs, homes, and love relationships? Does changing your handwriting feel like one too many items on your To Do List? Why not try some Bach flower essences? Larch boosts your self-esteem, Walnut helps you cope with upsetting changes, and Hornbeam gives you a shot of energy to take care of those Monday morning blues that can linger till Friday.

#6 Do you feel like Sherlock Holmes?

A word of caution here! While graphology is fun and informative, please keep your perceptions to yourself. Use this tool for *your* enlightenment, not anyone else's.

If you announce that you have been studying handwriting analysis, I guarantee you will be handed pages of scribbled signatures to analyze your friends' and their lovers' personalities. For your peace of mind and sanity, *please don't do it.* If you want to keep your friends, keep your mouth shut!

In the past, I foolishly suggested that my friends treat their delightfully eccentric lovers casually, rather than seriously. They always ignored me and moved in with, or married their latest love interests. When these relationships fell apart, guess who was blamed for not making them see the light?

#7 Build your intuition skills.

If you want to play the sleuth, like the Pink Panther, pay close attention to people who leave small gaps between specific letters in their handwriting. These people will always "know" when you tell a white lie.

You can become equally as intuitive by leaving a few gaps in your handwriting. When you do, heaven help anyone who tries to pull the wool over *your* eyes.

If you practice intuitive writing, you will always be the first to sense when a situation is heading south. Pay attention to these gut reactions! They are warning you to avoid dangerous situations such as driving on dark, unsafe streets, or drinking that second, multi-colored cocktail with the cherry on the top.

Most importantly they'll signal you when it's time to dump that bodacious lover for someone who has your best interests at heart.

Kila la kheri – which means good luck in Swahili.

* See References and Research

CHAPTER 5

I'M LATE, I'M LATE, FOR A VERY IMPORTANT DATE!

ARE YOU WASTING YOUR MOST PRECIOUS ASSET, TIME?

"I think you might do something better with the time"
Alice sighed wearily. —Lewis Carroll.

Imagine you are a contestant on a TV show, and there's $1 million on the line.

"Here's your million-dollar question," says the game show host. "What's the most commonly used word in the English language? Remember, the clock is ticking, and you have only sixty seconds to answer!"

What would you do?

Would you take a risk and try to win the $1 million prize? Or would you stutter, stammer, and miss your big chance?

And most importantly, what's the *correct* answer to this million-dollar question?*

It's *time!*

Tempus fugit – time flies. Time is our most precious asset, and it appears to be our most popular conversation topic, yet most of us have little or no expertise in effectively managing our time.

While our lives seem to get busier every year, time is finite and won't expand to meet our needs. Most of us end up *multitasking* to fit our long To Do lists into our day.

To top it all off, we struggle with social pressure to look skinny, even when we don't have time for the gym, and to act sexy, even if we're only getting six hours' sleep a night.

Yes. . . most of us multitaskers have had "beastly" days when we've missed a plane, boat, or train, and we are left like the White Rabbit in *Alice in Wonderland*, saying, "I'm late, I'm late, for a very important date!"

While being fashionably late is acceptable in some circles, in the corporate world being late can make all the difference between getting the business or getting "the boot."

I had a very important date as the in-studio guest on an early morning radio show in Fort Lauderdale, Florida. The station director was a terse and humorless man with a terrible temper.

"He's really nice, deep down," his assistant whispered confidentially.

"How deep?" I asked. "Do I have to dig down to Australia to find out?"

"Suzanne, be here at 6:00 a.m. sharp for the pre-show run through, and we go live at 7:00 a.m." said Mr. "Deep Down Nice." For me, a night owl, this was not an exciting preview of good times ahead; this was a predawn sentence.

"I'd rather climb Mount Everest in a blizzard than get up at 4:00 a.m. to go to work," I said, with dry British humor.

"You wanna see a blizzard, I'll show you a blizzard," he yelled. "If you're late for this show, there will such a blizzard in this station it will freeze your @#!@ off."

I wondered why this media mogul used such mad-dog language with so many foul four letter words. Was this some kind of status symbol? Certainly no one else at the station could say words like these and still get a paycheck on Friday.

Meanwhile I was reviewing the alarming prospect of arising before dawn to reach the radio station on time.

"Oh lawdy, that means a 4:00 a.m. wake-up call," I muttered.

Buzz zzz zzz zzz Buzz zzz zzz zzz

It seemed as if less than sixty seconds had passed between the time my head hit the pillow and my alarm was screeching like a bullet train as it tore under the English channel. It was 4:04 a.m. My eyelids felt as if they were glued together, and my furry-coated tongue was stuck to the roof of my mouth.

I made a mental note *never* to drink red wine the night before a 4:00 a.m. wake up call.

Half asleep, I stumbled into the kitchen, where I burned the toast along with my fingers. At this ethereal hour, my coordination was jumbled, and my logical left brain was still half asleep.

My snooty Persian cat, unused to any pre-dawn disturbances, gave a loud howl of disapproval, followed by an irate swish of her tail and quickly disappeared under the bed.

Three cups of Jamaican Blue Mountain coffee later, I was showered, caffeine spiked, and ready to start my day. . . .

"Take the toll road," my Floridian friends advised me. "It's a longer ride from Jupiter, but there'll be hardly any traffic at that time of day."

"Everything's going exactly as planned, which means I have plenty of time to check my e-mail before I head into the city," I muttered.

Wrong, wrong, wrong!

Twenty minutes later, I slid behind the wheel of my sleek silver convertible and switched on my favorite CD. Despite my Jamaican coffee jitters, and wild calypso music to keep me awake, everything went smoothly, almost too smoothly. . . .

Just as I was approaching the final toll plaza, a mere ten minutes from the radio station, my perfect planning went awry! Two Mexican farmers, driving a rusty red truck filled with ripe, green watermelons pulled into the exit lane ahead of me. With a loud bang and a belch of black smoke, their truck skidded sideways to a stop, completely blocking the entrance to the toll booth. It was 5:30 a.m.

After several attempts to restart the engine, which was making hiccupy coughing sounds as it poured out pungent black fumes, the fearless farmers clambered out of their truck to investigate the problem.

My body felt numb as they slowly opened the bonnet* and peered into the blackened engine. After two minutes that felt more like two hours, the sleepy tollbooth attendant shuffled toward the stalled truck.

"Excuse me, sir," I called out, trying not to sound panicky. "Can you help me get by? I'm running really late for a *show*."

He stared at me. At 5:30 a.m. I was *not* dressed for success. My blonde curly hair was blowing in the wind, and I was wearing a red, white and blue British T shirt and blue jeans. I looked like a late-night party goer, limping home in the early morning light, rather than a professional motivational speaker.

"Exactly what *kind* of show are we talking about?" he asked in a snippy, insulting tone.

"Sir, this is a radio show, not reality TV!" I said, feeling utterly helpless.

"I'm busy moving this truck, *lady*, so hold onto your horses," he snapped. For *lady* substitute another word that he was thinking, starting with the letter *B*.

Meanwhile, a chrome-yellow jeep, packed with smiling Australian surfers and their neon-colored surfboards, pulled in behind me. They were laughing and honking loudly, and the noise was getting on my already-jangled nerves.

The minutes passed excruciatingly slowly, and I started to sweat profusely. The surfers stopped honking and scrambled out of their jeep to assist the harried-looking farmers.

"What's the problem, mate? We've got some waves to catch," they joked.

An international mechanical conference took place between the American tollbooth attendant, the Australian surfers, and the Mexican farmers, as an *eternity* passed!

Finally, a United Nations referendum was made to push the stalled truck through the tollbooth. The Mexicans and the Australians heaved and hollered, while the American tollbooth attendant held up his hand to alert any oncoming traffic.

At last, the watermelon truck was safely on a grassy bank beside the road, leaving a clear passage for my escape. I breathed a sigh of relief and revved up my car, ready to speed ahead.

"Wait a minute, *wait a minute*," shouted Mr. Grumpy.

So much time had elapsed during this international incident that it was time for a shift change. Ahead of me, a weary-looking cashier was waiting patiently to step into the traffic lanes. It was like the "changing of the guard" ceremony at Buckingham Palace except, on this hot and muggy Florida morning, the only Brit for miles around had completely lost her impeccable British manners.

"You've gotta be kidding," I screamed, as Mr. Grumpy stood in front of the barrier to stop me and the boisterous Australians from rolling forward.

"Hold on, guys. Let my co-worker pass."

The bleary-eyed cashier shuffled toward his tollbooth carrying a heavy metal tray jam-packed with silver coins.

"Watch out," I yelled, but I was just wasting my breath. The watermelon truck had left a pool of oil on the street. He didn't see this over his enormous tray until it was too late. He slipped and slithered on the thick black slick as he struggled to stay upright. But it was no use! His legs went flying from under him, and hundreds of silver coins flew into the air.

"OK, OK, Miss Superstar, you'll just have to wait a bit longer," Mr. Grumpy growled, as he slapped his hand on my car bonnet in exasperation.

Time passed excruciatingly slowly as the Mexicans and the Australians returned to the tollbooth to gather up the sticky money. By now, I was having difficulty breathing, and my chest was in a viselike grip.

"Sir, I'm on a tight deadline for a *live* show. Can you please let me through?"

My voice was raspy from stress and a lack of sleep. I glanced in my rearview mirror. Big mistake! I saw a frazzled-looking face staring back at me. My clammy shirt was now clinging to my belly, and my naturally curly hair had turned into a frizzy afro from the sweltering heat and humidity. I looked like a blonde version of Bob Marley.

"So, who are you *now*, Katie Couric?" asked Mr. Grumpy. This was clearly not the appropriate time to argue that Katie Couric was a TV anchorwoman, not a radio talk-show host.

I searched for my cell phone and dialed the station, but every line was busy. They were probably dialing out, trying to reach me, so I handed my cell phone to Mr. Grumpy.

"Sir, would you dial the radio station and tell them I *died* last night and you are shipping my body back to London. Because right now, I might as well be *dead*."

Mr. Grumpy, like the queen of England, was *not amused*.

Finally, all the coins were collected, and I was waved through the tollbooth, dripping with sweat.

As with all time-management-hell days, my hell was not over, and I was about to burn.

I drove like a bat out of hell toward the radio station until I encountered yet another time management phenomenon.

New to the Sunshine State, I'd forgotten that Florida is known as the Venice of the Americas. In Florida, roads often double as bridges - drawbridges. Without any warning, my road was turning into a drawbridge that was opening rapidly.

"Not now, God! Not *today*," I shrieked.

Yes, now and today! With a loud clanging of bells and flashing of lights, the drawbridge swung open, leaving me on the wrong side of the tracks. Can you believe it? I was actually calculating whether I could jump the void like James Bond.

Seven sailboats passed under the drawbridge. Carefree holidaymakers waved at the exasperated drivers, who sat with gritted teeth behind swaying red barriers. I wanted to scream, "Caramba, can't you go any faster. I'm late, I'm late, for a very important date."

Time passed as languidly as a lunar eclipse while I was experiencing sharp, stabbing pains in my chest. It was time for some emergency stress management. I rummaged in my purse for my bottle of Rescue Remedy and took a big slug.

The pre-dawn traffic had been replaced by early morning rush-hour traffic. I fought the panic rising in my chest as I attempted to conjure up some plausible excuse.

"Could these chest pains be a premonition of my impending doom?" I asked myself. "Should I cut my losses and run, rather than face some foulmouthed denigration from the station director?"

No matter how stressful the circumstances, I've learned that taking small risks always boosts my self-confidence, while quitting or running away, leaves me feeling disappointed and regretful.

I took some long, deep breaths and summoned every ounce of courage in my body. "This drive-to-work show will go better than expected," I said, trusting that my guardian angels were early risers.

I ran into the radio station with only five minutes before we were "live". The station director was shrieking in his office like a raging bull elephant. I heard my name screamed amidst a string of colorful adjectives and some heavy desk pounding.

The receptionist looked ashen faced. "Suzanne, we've been trying to reach you for hours." She hesitated before buzzing me in, as if I were Anne Boleyn and she was sending me to an untimely death.

The producer gave me one of those *"If looks could kill, you would be dead"* kind of looks. There was no time to explain; the countdown light was blinking, 3–2–1 and we were *live*.

"Did you oversleep?" the producer asked, after the show was a big success and formerly frayed tempers were slowly reweaving together.

"Actually, I was learning TM," I said.

"Aha! So you do Transcendental Meditation?" he said. "*Now* I understand. You must teach me! I need to learn TM to cope with the stress of this job."

I didn't want to disappoint him and tell him that in this case, TM meant *time management*. Besides, I was thinking, that's not such a bad idea. I *should* learn Transcendental Meditation before agreeing to another 4:00 a.m. wake-up call.

How about you? Do you want your day to be *heavenly* rather than *hellish*? Then try some of these creative time-management tools for yourself.

If you have a tendency to procrastinate, like me, and arrive late for that very important date, your clients, colleagues, and prospective love partners will have formed an opinion about you that is set in stone, and you will have to chisel away for years before you can change it.

In the business world, the phrase "better late than never" is inaccurate. If you arrive late for that very important business date, like the White Rabbit, you'll be left down the rabbit hole. Chances are you'll *never* be given another chance to display your sensational new product, bid on that substantial contract, or sign the sales deal of the century.

RISKS AND REWARDS
TO SAVE TIME & MONEY

#1 Turn hellish days into heavenly ones.
Ask yourself, "What's the best use of my time right now?" This question gives you clarity in the midst of confusion. Despite all the chaos around you, you *do* have choices. You can choose to focus on your long-term goals and dreams, or you can choose to waste your precious time, worrying.

When you ask this question, you will begin to sense, or instinctively feel your answer. You may be guided to take a class, start writing a book, or spend an hour strolling in the park. The more you ask this question, the more you will be guided.

One night I was driving home, dog-tired after a dismal day. Some days, when *we* are on time, others are not, and I felt frustrated about all the time I'd wasted.

So I asked, "What's the best use of the rest of my day?"

Go to the local supermarket, popped into my head.

"But if I go *there*, I'll buy chocolate mint ice cream and *eat* it, so that's not such a great idea," I argued.

Go anyway, I was guided.

At the entrance to the store was a stand displaying the latest *TIME* magazine. Earlier that morning I'd been asked to give a speech on risk-taking at a retreat for women in business. The *TIME* lead story focused on innovative female CEO's. Those three pages save me hours of research time.

While the start of my day had been hellish, the end of my day was heavenly. I savored my chocolate mint ice cream and celebrated. Thanks to asking and acting on my gut responses, all the time I'd wasted had been made up before the day's end.

#2 It's never too late to restart your day.

If you ate french fries at lunch and Twinkies at tea time, your day *isn't* completely ruined. You can take a risk and restart your day at any moment you choose.

Say out loud, "I'm going to restart this day, right now. This is going to be one of my best days ever."

Once you shift your perception of time to understand that you can restart your day at any moment you choose, you can relax and spend the rest of your day acting constructively. Try it, and you will be astonished how *stuck* situations will turn around. My restarted days have always been my most successful days.

#3 Take one step toward order every day.

How much time do you spend searching for your car keys, your credit cards, or your cell phone?

If you organize your clothes on one day, and clean out a drawer or find a permanent home for your car keys and cell phone on another, in one month your life will become more orderly. Try color-coordinating your closet. This one small step makes any 6:00 a.m. dressing dilemma seem effortless.

#4 Natural remedies for time management.

Many of us feel overwhelmed by the number of tasks on our To Do list. Feeling overwhelmed zaps our energy and, yes, makes us late for that very important date.

Try the Bach flower essence Elm to soothe those "I've too much to do and too little time to do it in" days. Elm will help you to handle multiple tasks with ease.*

#5 Time out for creative time management.
Set aside ten minutes every morning and evening for precious personal time. Use these minutes to start and end your day in a positive frame of mind.

Think of this as *bookending* your day. Remind yourself that "The first and last ten minutes of the day belong to me." If your life is impossibly busy, you may have to get up ten minutes earlier and go to bed ten minutes later, but *it's worth it*.

If you have a tough day ahead, play some music that uplifts your spirits. If you feel discouraged, try Billy Idol's "Dancing with Myself" and spin around as you brew your coffee and brush your teeth. If you feel stressed and anxious, soothe your mind by listening to Mozart or Steven Halpern's "Spectrum Suite."*

At the close of your day, give thanks for all the good things that happened. Maybe someone gave you a compliment, or you found the perfect sweater and the perfect parking space. Whatever we focus on expands. The more we focus on the good, the more we will attract good things into our lives. It's the Law of Attraction.

Here's some food for thought: The happiest and most successful people I know take a sixty-minute time out every single day. They spend this hour focusing on their goals and dreams and sustaining a constant stream of appreciation for all that is right in their world.

Are you are hell-bent on transforming your life - really fast? Then follow their lead and get up one hour earlier, or go to bed one hour later, for 365 days. The pain is *temporary,* but the results are *permanent.* I guarantee your life will change, and you will feel clearheaded and creative, even on the craziest of days.

#6 Take charge of phone calls and texts.

Forget your knee-jerk reactive response to answer your phone, return texts, and send e-mails. You are setting a precedent that you are always available ASAP. In the next few months, as your personal transformation unfolds, you will be far too busy to be "on call" 24/7.

Unless this is your beloved, your boss, or the VIP client who covers your bills, return calls *after* you have completed the critical tasks for the day.

#7 Find the purpose and plan for your life.

When you discover the purpose and plan for your life, you will never, ever, waste another minute. You will feel so energized and fired up that you will want to make every minute count.

Are you still searching for your life's purpose? *Most* of us are! Why not take a twenty-minute creative walk? (Chapter 6). This is a great way to find your true path in life and experience creative miracles.

Don't be disappointed if you aren't given the winning lottery ticket numbers, or the title of your best-selling book on your creative walk. This is a time for sewing creative seeds. Fabulous ideas will flow into your mind later, usually at hugely inconvenient moments, while you are making love, making an important phone call, or making high speed lane changes on I95.

This is not an appropriate time to say, "Hold on a minute, while I jot down this fabulous idea!" You will either madden your mate or end up in front of a magistrate for reckless driving.

In closing – please don't play the White Rabbit, assuming you can squeeze one more task into your incredibly busy day. Learning to say "no" is never selfish. It's an essential part of setting boundaries and standing up for the new, self-confident you.

Today, why not take a risk and arrive at your appointments *early* rather than late?

Carry this book or a personal project with you at all times. This creative preparedness allows you to spend precious moments focusing on your *own* goals and dreams, rather than someone else's.

* See References and Research

CHAPTER 6

THE CREATIVE WALK

HOW TO MANIFEST CREATIVE MIRACLES AND FIND YOUR LIFE'S PURPOSE

"Miracles come from a change in consciousness,
not a change in circumstances."
—Michael Rann & Elizabeth Rann Arrott

"You should come to my *Face Your Fears* workshop. It will test your courage and self-confidence as well as clearing any creative blocks. By the way, I *sense* that you really *need* this," said my divinely handsome date as he held my hand over the dinner table.

What else did he sense about me, I wondered - that I was having too much *sugar* and way too little *sex*?

Up to that moment I'd been feeling just fine. I was having dinner in a beautiful beachfront restaurant in Santa Barbara with a drop-dead, gorgeous man. Christov was a tall, blond-haired Swede, who looked like Fabio, the hunk in the *I can't believe it's not butter* commercial. But now that dinner was over, he was staring into my eyes and sensing things about me that needed to be changed.

"Couldn't I have just *one* romantic dinner, God, without it having to be a character building experience?" I muttered.

Despite my misgivings, forty-eight hours later on a bright and blustery day in southern California, I stepped from a windswept sandy beach into a serene yoga studio with polished wood floors, paddle fans like swirling palm trees, and tinkling Tibetan bells.

I was joined by an eclectic group of six-pack-abs surfers, long-haired Swedish yogis, and bold adventure seekers for my first *Face Your Fears* workshop.

"This'll be a piece of cake for *me*," I said as I scribbled my name on the legal release document.

After all, I'd camped in the African jungle, zip-lined over the Costa Rican rain forest, and ridden a camel across a remote Middle Eastern desert.

"It can't be any scarier than *that*, can it?" I asked myself.

I was about to find out.

"Welcome," said Christov softly, shaking his long blond mane, mesmerizing *all* the women and, I suspect, most of the good-looking men gathered around him.

"On this sunny Saturday afternoon, you are about to face your deepest, darkest fears. First take off your shoes and stretch out your toes. We will start by doing some deep-breathing exercises to release any anxiety and stress."

Just as we were feeling soothed and serene, Christov jolted us back to reality. With a wild flourish, he unfurled a shiny black tarpaulin the size of two bed sheets and flung it on the polished pine floor.

Next, he hauled in two bulky sacks of broken glass and poured these spiky pieces onto the slick black surface. A wave of panic swept through my body as I watched this bloodcurdling scene unfolding.

"He's joking, right? Surely he isn't going to ask us to step on this broken glass in our bare feet?" I asked an equally horrified classmate.

"I've heard of walking on hot coals, but isn't that something that Native American medicine men perform after months of praying and fasting?" he replied.

"Maybe this is the Californian version of *Eat, Pray, Love!*"

But I hadn't prayed *or* loved that morning and was now *fervently* wishing that I had.

I had, however, eaten a large lobster salad for lunch - rather foolishly, in retrospect. The mere idea of stepping on broken glass was already creating a churning, burning sensation in my stomach.

Clearly, on this day, I had bitten off more than I could chew!

Sixteen men and women shuffled nervously to the back of the room and declined to participate any further.

Christov addressed the foolhardy few of us remaining.

"It's time to take a risk and face your innermost fears! In order for you to walk across this field of glass without cutting your feet, you must move mindfully, letting go of any and all fears."

Alrighty then, exactly how are you supposed to do that? the left, logical side of my brain was asking, while simultaneously giving me warning signals to run out the door while the going was good.

"Most of us are bogged down by the stress of our daily lives. When we feel stressed, we disconnect from our brains' creative ability to send us sensational ideas and protect us in times of danger," Christov pronounced in a booming, sonorous voice.

I wondered why he was speaking so loudly when the room had become so deathly quiet you could have heard a pin drop.

"Stress dulls our sensory awareness and makes us cranky, critical, and even chronically depressed. Stress plays havoc with our creativity as well as *annihilating our sex drive*," he said forcefully.

His last statement surfaced a loud gasp of shock from the back of the room. I didn't turn around to see who had received a lightning flash of recognition regarding his or her sex drive, or rather the *lack* of it.

Besides, I was trying, rather unsuccessfully, to appear serene and not the least bit sex deprived, while Christov continued to give us last minute instructions that felt ridiculously like our last rites. Was this how they felt in the TV show *Survivor*? I wondered, as I mentally deleted any foolish ideas I'd been harboring about auditioning for the show.

"Today I want you to step boldly across this broken glass, knowing that any fearful thoughts in your head will show up as sharp pains in your feet," Christov continued.

I didn't need to feel sharp pains in my feet; I was already feeling them in the pit of my stomach!

His controversial ideas didn't shock me. I'd read dozens of books that explored the innovative concept that our thoughts create our reality.

"But I'm *not* the *Survivor* type!" I exclaimed. "I'm not prepared to test my personal fear factor by walking on broken glass, trembling in front of my peers."

There was a murmur of agreement around the room, but it seemed nobody was brave enough to make the first move. We were all assessing the risks, along with our physical stamina, before standing up.

After a few highly charged moments, a couple of well-built jocks, with muscular thighs, six-pack abs, and well-callused soles, stepped boldly across the green glass field in front of me.

"Obviously, there is nothing wrong with *our* sex drive," they said, while the rest of the group laughed nervously.

I was the *only* one who wasn't laughing. I was worrying about something so much more important than my libido - my *feet*.

"Why didn't I postpone my pedicure?" I moaned. My feet were smooth and buffed, without a single callus to protect me.

A teenage girl, wearing a skimpy bra, a silver stud in her belly button, and a pair of strategically ripped jeans stepped bravely onto the broken glass in front of me. Halfway across, she became paralyzed with fear and had to be carried off.

"OK, Suzanne, now it's your turn," said Christov.

But my knees were knocking, and my legs were quivering. There was so much tension in the air you could have cut it with a knife.

I took a long, deep breath and my first tentative step. The hairs on my head were standing on end, while I could swear that my heart was standing still. The crunching sound as I placed my right foot gingerly on the broken glass seemed to echo in my brain and around the hushed room.

I had one foot in the danger zone and one foot in the safety zone, and I was immobilized by sheer terror! After years of taking small, manageable risks, some days I attempted seemingly insurmountable ones.

Yes, this was one of those days . . . .

My brain was sending me mixed signals.

Step back and say you've changed your mind. Once you've put both feet on the glass, you're committed, said my left, logical brain.

Go on; give it a try, my right, creative brain said encouragingly.

It's a great story, but you don't have to risk getting your feet cut to shreds to write it, my left brain retorted.

Before logic could take over, I put both feet on the glass. My legs were shaking as I took my first faltering steps. It felt as if I were climbing the north face of the Eiger in my bare feet.

Fear surfaced immediately as a choking sensation in my throat. A split second later, I felt a corresponding sharp stabbing pain in my feet. Aha! Is this what those gurus were alluding to? Could our thoughts *really* create our reality?

"Close your eyes and let go of your fears," Christov whispered. "Whenever you feel good, you are healing. Don't be afraid, Suzanne; we all have something to heal. Whether it's a loss of finances, failed love relationships, or lack of creative flow."

O lawdy, how did he know so much about me? I wondered. In a few words he'd captured my three greatest fears. Was he a modern-day Marquis de Sade as well as a mystical intuitive?

Like many creative professionals, I was having one of those dreaded *dry* spells. My dominant fear that day was that my artistic talents had disappeared like the setting sun, never to arise again.

I closed my eyes and asked to let go of my fears and make a fresh start, no matter how many risks that entailed.

When I opened my eyes, I was astonished to find that my feet felt light as a feather, as if I were walking across my favorite rocky beach in Hawaii.

As I crossed the green glass glacier, there was a loud burst of applause from the group.

"How did it feel?" everyone asked.

"It was *extraordinary*. Who knew I could do this and not be scared to death? Why can't I live this fearlessly every single day?" I asked.

"That's the whole point; you can," Christov said. "It just takes practice."

Three women and seven men, like a team of shaggy Sherpas, crossed the treacherous glass glacier that day without experiencing a *single scratch.*

This was a pivotal day in my life. I danced on the edge of my fears and defeated them. After this rite of passage, my creative talents flowed like warm rain, and I began coaching artists, writers, and women in recovery to facilitate a creative breakthrough in their lives.*

I won't suggest you walk on broken glass! It's far too dangerous, and I'll *never* do this again. Besides, if you have a high stress job in the city, you already know how this feels.

Instead, why not take a break from all your worries and take a twenty-minute creative walk before breakfast, or before bedtime? You will be surprised how a short creative walk can reduce your stress, clarify your life's purpose, and revamp your sex life, should you need it!

While it's professionally unacceptable to have a bodacious attitude at work, unless you are the boss, you can strut your stuff with as much attitude as you can muster on your creative stroll!

Whether you stroll or strut, if you want to be more creative there is only one criterion. For twenty minutes you must leave all your worries behind.

Most of us want to reinvent our lives as happy and more fulfilling. Yet when push comes to shove, we shake our heads and say, "It would take a *miracle* to change *my* life."

My question to you is not *if*, but *when* would you like that to happen?

Are you ready to experience a miracle in your life? If so, then this is the perfect time to ask. The dictionary definition of *miracle* is an event that appears inexplicable by the laws of nature. Whether you believe in miracles or not, all of us have experienced, or *know* someone who has experienced, something that is impossible, illogical, or inexplicable.

Here's how to ask for *your* miracle. When you take your creative stroll, flood your body with a sense of appreciation for all the abundance in your world. It doesn't matter whether it's for the leaves on the trees, the stars in the sky, or the people, places, and possessions in your life.

Imagine how your life would change if you were more creative. Here are just three possibilities . . .

You could reduce your stress and feel more alert and alive.

You could find your purpose in life, along with a more fulfilling career.

You could find the perfect mate for your creative soul.

Hold on to those feelings of having *one* of these dreams come true. It's like opening a doorway for the Universe to flow miracles into your life.

A miracle does not appear and disappear. Every time we speak about the inexplicable events, or miracles, that have occurred in our lives, we become *miracle workers*. Our miracles grow and expand as our stories inspire others, who have lost all hope, to ask for a miracle in their *own* lives.

So what's holding you back? Are you worried that your friends or co-workers would make disparaging comments if you took a twenty-minute creative walk at lunchtime?

If you said *Yes,* let me ask you this:

Don't you have enough people telling you what to do, what to say, and how to think every moment of your day?

The purpose of your creative walk is to let go of all fear and limitations and tap into infinite creative ideas that can change your life.

As you head out the door, here's one final thought: What will you be doing one year from today?

Will you be doing the same old same old, or will you have transformed yourself into someone who has clarity, creativity, and a sense of purpose?

All it takes is a twenty-minute creative walk to let go of your worries and *walk* your true path in life.

RISKS & REWARDS
TO MANIFEST CREATIVE MIRACLES

#1 Use quiet time for creative inspiration.
"But I don't have time for *that*," is the usual excuse.

"Boosting your creativity will take some time, focus, and planning."

"Exactly how *much* time are we talking about?" I'm asked.

For those logical, analytical folks, here are the simple facts.

In the next 365 days you will have 8,760 hours to transform yourself. If you take a twenty-minute creative walk every day, it will only take 121 of those hours, leaving you 8,589 hours to do everything else. With all the vim and vigor your creative walk generates, wouldn't this be time well invested?

Tomorrow, why not take a risk and spend twenty minutes walking toward a bright, creative future, with a light step and an even lighter heart?

#2 If you're feeling good, you're healing.

Most of us spend half our day worrying about the past and feeling anxious about the future. The purpose of your creative walk is to break this worry habit and get in touch with your creative side and your heart's desires.

How long is it since you spent twenty minutes without worrying? If you aren't worrying about your own "stuff," most likely you are worrying about someone else's. Stop it; please stop it, for twenty minutes a day.

As you switch off your stressed-out brain and switch on your feel-good brain, you'll be astonished how calm, clearheaded, and creative you can feel.

#3 Stimulate your sensory awareness.

If you walk outdoors, move mindfully. Touch a leaf, a tree, or a rough stone wall and feel the texture with your fingertips. Listen to the sounds around you. Can you hear birds singing or dogs barking?

Take a sip of water. Is it ice cold or lukewarm, sparkly or flat? Pop a peppermint or a slice of lemon into your mouth. Savor the taste and the tingling sensation on your tongue. These simple sensory exercises will tune up your creative brain so it can send you simply "smashing" ideas, as we say in England.

But what if it's stormy weather? Try walking in a garden center and surround yourself with flowering plants and trees for twenty minutes. Or stroll through a farmer's market and touch, taste, and smell the fresh fruits and vegetables.

Try walking in a tree-lined labyrinth,* an art gallery, or on a windswept sandy beach. It's best to walk in silence if you want to stimulate your creative flow. Focus on your sensory awareness rather than your worries.

#4 Take a few steps backward.

Yes, people will look at you and wonder what you are doing. That's your risk for the day. Seeking and finding the purpose and plan for your life sometimes means stepping back and reviewing what's worked for you and what hasn't. Pausing and taking a few steps back on your creative walk gives your heart and soul the time and space to redirect you.

#5 Having fun is a creative activity.

"Are you having enough fun?"

When I ask this question at my book signings, most people will shake their heads and say *No*. Did you know the average four-year-old laughs three hundred times a day, while a forty-year-old laughs only fourteen times.*

The solution to our doldrums is not Valium. The answer is fun and laughter.

Laughing and having fun stimulates our creative flow. It's the Law of Attraction. The more we laugh, the more we attract upbeat creative ideas and positive people into our lives.

Laughter is not only infectious, it helps fight off infections. Laughter releases feel-good hormones called endorphins so we feel better, sleep better, and feel less stressed.

While holidays are wonderful times to enjoy fun and laughter, many American workers will not take time away from their jobs this year.* This means that if we are to find and keep our creative edge, we must add more fun to our *daily* lives.

Why not add some fun to your creative walk by strutting like a rock star? Try swaggering to the song "Moves Like Jagger" by Maroon 5. It's guaranteed to lift your spirits and make you laugh.

When your twenty minutes are up, give yourself a treat. How about sipping a fluffy cappuccino, renting a funny movie, or buying a bunch of daisies (happy flowers) for your home or desk?

#6 How can I stop my negative thinking?

White Chestnut is a Bach flower essence that helps quiet those worrisome thoughts that block our creative flow.

Taking long, deep breaths as you walk helps to clear and oxygenate the brain. It's free and it works.

#7 What if you can't walk?

Three years ago at 1:11 on a Monday morning, my laissez-faire attitude toward life was shattered in a split second. I was injured in an accident and rushed to the hospital with my leg swollen to three times its normal size.

"This can't be happening! Any minute now, I'll wake up and this will all have been a bad dream," I sobbed. I struggled to get a grasp on reality as paramedics pushed me at high speed into the ice-cold emergency room.

Before I could ask questions, I was gagging at the smell of industrial-strength disinfectant and gasping in shock as a team of stone-faced doctors and nurses surrounded my bed.

Sickly green curtains were drawn around my bed like sabers rattling a death knell while I was poked and prodded in every orifice.

"You're hurting me," I tried to protest, but the words would not come out of my mouth. Moments later I was turned into a human pin cushion as needles were jabbed into my arms and legs, and I was hooked up to an imposing IV pole.

"What are you giving me?" I mumbled, struggling to maintain consciousness.

"One bag is a powerful antibiotic to save your leg, and the other bag is morphine for the pain," my surgeon said matter-of-factly.

The next forty-eight hours were a wild ride. For the past twenty years I'd taken nothing stronger than an aspirin. Now I had enough pain killers pumped into me to start my own pharmacy!

Once the swelling began to subside and my brain was no longer drugged senseless, I asked about my future health and happiness.

"How soon will be able to go dancing again?" I asked my surgeon.

"You won't be dancing for a *very* long time and maybe *never*," he said, shaking his head. You've got to stay on intravenous antibiotics and keep that leg elevated for the next few weeks. Then I'm sending you for physical therapy. It could take months till you are back to normal."

"You've got to be kidding," I said, "I'm going to walk out of here *this week*."

He smiled benevolently. If I were a dog he would have patted me on the head and said, "Down girl!"

In a split second I'd been catapulted into uncharted territory. For years I had traveled the world, helping my clients recover from injuries, surgeries, and life's stressful challenges, and coaching them to find a renewed sense of power and purpose for their lives.

Now the tables had been turned. This time *I* was the one facing a long-term recovery following a life-threatening injury.

Two hours earlier I'd been wearing a pink cotton dress and dancing to a lively calypso band. "Don't forget, Suzanne! Save the last dance for me," my date had said as we took a breather.

Now I was wearing a beige-striped hospital gown that barely covered my dignity and wondering if I'd already danced my very last dance.

Battling anxiety and depression at the thought of being bedbound for what seemed like an eternity, I searched desperately for ways to accelerate my healing process.

Here's what worked for me. . . .

I took a mental creative walk for twenty minutes a day.

I closed my eyes and pictured myself in one of my favorite places.

The place I chose was the magical, mystical island of Patmos, Greece.* Patmos is a beautiful island, where St. John wrote the Book of Revelation in a cave overlooking the ocean. We were both exiles. He had been exiled to Patmos, while I had been exiled to the solitude and stillness of my hospital bed. As I was seeking solutions, and revelations, about my own healing, for me, Patmos was the perfect place.

I pictured myself strolling beside the harbor as the sun set over the deep blue sea and lights sparkled on the hillside. For twenty minutes I let go of all my anger, pain, and frustration and immersed myself in the sensations of this memory. I recalled the sweet scent of flowers in the air, the pungent aroma of roasted coffee, and the salty taste of goat cheese on warm, crusty bread.

After my mental creative walk I felt more optimistic about my body's ability to heal quickly. Five days later, I defied my doctor's diagnosis and walked out of the hospital unaided.

"It's a *miracle*," everyone declared.

"Some miracles aren't supernatural; they are created," I replied.

Here's the good news: You don't have to operate out of despair anymore if you are in pain, and you don't have to be mobile to experience a creative miracle. All you need is an active imagination. Think of all the beautiful places you've seen and write them down. Each day, vividly imagine yourself in one of these places.

Your creative imagination is enhanced by your senses, so take time to recall all the colors and sounds, along with those scrumptious tastes and smells.

Whenever we focus our thoughts on something wonderful for twenty minutes a day, even if we are bedbound, or in chronic pain, we can generate a bright healing energy that attracts extraordinary outcomes to us.

The kind of extraordinary outcomes that some of us call *miracles!*

So what are you waiting for? Slip on your walking shoes, and let's take a creative walk together toward an absolutely fabulous future that's jam-packed with the impossible, illogical, and inexplicable experiences that *I* like to call *miracles.*

* See References and Research

St. George's books will be available on CD shortly so you can laugh along with her as you take your creative walk.

CHAPTER 7

ANTI-AGING SECRETS FOR CITY SLICKERS

HOW TO LOOK YOUNGER, FEEL BETTER, AND LOSE WEIGHT

"It's so much easier to *do* good, than to *be* good."
—B.C. Forbes

It's 8:30 Monday morning, and your knees are knocking. . .

No, you are not about to get fired, but you *are* about to have another kind of fire lit under you!

You are sitting in an ice-cold office wearing last week's newspaper, which is now euphemistically called a surgical gown. Even though the temperature is freezing, you are sweating bullets. You glance around, hoping to see something, anything, to cheer you up, but all you see is colored drawings of carcasses and a skeleton hanging lifelessly in the corner.

"It looks like my number is up," you mutter.

Your doctor strides in, but he is not smiling: He is *frowning*. He tosses a sheaf of test results on his desk.

Your heart skips a beat when you see that most of them have bright red warning stickers.

"I'm sorry to tell you that your results are *not* looking good. Your blood pressure is sky high, your bone density is low, and your cholesterol is through the roof. You have severe acid reflux disease, so your digestion is shot! What worries me most is that that you are diabetic, which is bad news as your heart is weak.

"I am sending you to a cardiac specialist, who will prescribe medication for your heart disease, high cholesterol, and diabetes.

"I know this comes as a *terrible* shock, so I'm giving you a prescription for some powerful anti-depressants to steady your nerves," your doctor says in a chilly, unnerving tone. "But if you don't quit smoking, start exercising, and lose twenty pounds ASAP, you are a ticking time bomb ready to explode."

Caramba! Until that sword of Damocles fell, you were unstoppable. Those TV ads showing the terrifying outcomes of smoking, drinking, and overeating didn't apply to *you*. You were a modern-day superwoman or superman until you were told, Change your eating and smoking habits, or you will die *sooner* rather than later.

Many of us will be clobbered by a life-changing diagnosis like this and bitterly wish we'd taken better care of ourselves. And, yes, that includes *me*.

This can be a *do or die* moment, when clients and friends call me and say, "O lawdy, my days are numbered! Can you believe it, I just received a letter from a funeral service asking if I wanted to pre-pay my burial expenses? Am I being given some last-ditch warning from the other side?"

"It often takes a scary diagnosis to motivate us to change. While facing our own mortality is never easy, when it is spelled out in days it can come as a big shock.

"30,000 days, or eighty-five years is the healthy lifespan we can enjoy, and beyond, if we learn how to eat right, detox our bodies and manage our stress.

"30,000 days seems so little time, when we do the math and figure out how much time we have left. These numbers can have us pulling on our jogging shoes and running to the juice bar on the way to the gym.

"Here's the bad news. The C.D.C. longevity statistics don't give us that long. On average, most of us will have a few thousand days less.

"OK, I really get it. Because once I hit fifty, my body started falling apart," you may sigh.

"How stressed are you right now on a scale of 1 – 10?" I always ask.

"Jeepers creepers, I'm an 11."

"That bad, eh? Did you know that almost 90 percent of doctors' visits are for stress-related issues? Stress in our bodies, or inflammation, is often caused by the food we eat.

"It's a surprisingly well-kept secret that refined sugar and its conjugated counterpart, high-fructose corn syrup, can cause inflammation that damages our hearts. Most of us aren't aware of the dangers of a high-sugar diet, which is why two-thirds of us are wired, tired, or overweight."

"So that means no sweets or desserts for whatever's *left* of my life?" you ask.

"No way! It's time to demystify the food/stress connection. This isn't rocket science; it's simple food consciousness. It's not like the movie, *The French Connection*, where if you get it wrong, *you die*. It's the *Food/Stress Connection*, where if you get it right, you will lose weight, feel great, and live a longer, happier, life."

In today's business world many of us work a fifty- or sixty-hour week. Long hours and job stress can make us so jittery that we ditch our get-slim-quick diet and switch into survival mode. Our food/stress connection can reach a crisis point on Monday mornings.

Do you attend mandatory Monday morning meetings from hell? If you answered *Yes*, then most likely you spend your Sundays worrying about your Mondays, especially if you are in sales, and haven't made your quota.

But here's the *really* bad news: Your Sunday of worry will have caused an inflammatory response in your body long before you walk through the office door!

As for your boss, most likely he spends *his* Sundays dreading Mondays too. When you say a cheery "Hello," does his gloomy demeanor remind you of the Grim Reaper sending shockwaves through your system? Or maybe it's his clenched jaw and tight-lipped expression that triggers your stomach to tighten in knots?

"Don't tell me he's about to announce my biggest accounts have died and gone to heaven, and my career will follow shortly?" you worry and wonder.

These stressful notions can send you scurrying to the snack machine, where you throw caution to the wind! You swallow a high-fructose-corn-syrup coffee, quickly followed by a chocolate-covered donut, so you won't look *quite* as queasy as you feel.

Finally, the meeting starts and your accounts are safe, at least for another week, so you eat another donut to celebrate. When the meeting runs into lunchtime, your boss orders pizza and sodas. You drink *two* sugary colas, because the pepperoni pizza was so salty, and by 2:00 p.m., you are on the phone, calling the pharmacy for a refill of your acid-reflux pills.

Back at your desk, you have eight hours' work to do and only four hours to do it in, so you call your sweetheart to say, "I'm sorry, honey, I have to work late tonight."

All you get is a snippy reminder that its your *anniversary* and you have dinner reservations. . . .

Is it any wonder that Monday mornings are prime time for heart attacks?*

Any stress overload, whether it's career, or family-related, combined with a sugar overload, can thrust our bodies into the inflammation danger zone. Sugar overload is a major factor in obesity, arthritis, heart disease, depression, diabetes, and premature aging, says Dr. Stephen Sinatra, co-author of *Sugar Shock*.

So how can we tell what's good and what's bad for us? What causes us to age rapidly, and what keeps us slim and trim?

Like a modern-day Ponce de Léon, I searched the world for that elusive fountain of youth. To my surprise, I discovered it's not in some magic potion from the Andes or some genie in Aladdin's lamp.

How we age is a combination of five factors: our stress levels, hydration levels, our family genes, the freshness of our food, and our ability to cope with life's constant stress!

While we cannot change our family genes, we can make simple changes that can have an immediate impact our health and looks. There's no need to move to a mountaintop in Tibet, or tie our bodies into knots, to make a big difference.

Here's a life-changing question for you:

Are you still sitting on the fence about taking a few risks? Did you know that taking two daily risks develops your stress-coping skills? As stress is the #1 reason we age faster, and get sicker quicker, why not give risk-taking a shot?

Risk-taking builds your courage, improves your self-image, and creates rock-solid self-confidence. Risk-taking gives you an opportunity to take back your power and re-build your resilience. Problems that would have caused endless sleepless nights in your pre-risk days simply become "stuff" you can take in your stride.

My first indicator of the sugar/stress connection came dramatically when my hair began falling out in handfuls. I would cry every time I took a shower and saw my hair disappearing down the drain.

My close friends tried to comfort me as my deteriorating marriage spiraled into the divorce courts.

"It's just *stress*! Once your divorce is over, your hair will grow back, *you'll see*."

My divorce dragged on. I left the congested air of London for the clean mountain air of Switzerland, but my hair continued to fall out. I felt like an English sheep dog shedding her winter coat. I found blonde hair on my couch, in my car, and on my kitchen floor.

"I've got to stop losing my hair before I look like an alien from Mars!" I sobbed into my bathroom mirror. I was frantic to find a solution before I became completely bald. I spent months poring over British medical journals, and I consulted eminent Swiss doctors about the correlation between my high-stress job and the handfuls of hair in my shower.

"Sugar can trigger depression, premature aging, weight gain, wrinkles, tooth loss, *and* hair loss," these Swiss doctors told me. That last item made me drop my Cadbury's chocolate biscuit in dismay.

It was tough enough dealing with the back-stabbing drama of my divorce. Now, it seemed, I was about to become the real life Bridget, in *Bridget Jones's Diary*. I was facing the hideous prospect of becoming *single, fat, wrinkled, toothless, and bald* !

I was on an emotional roller coaster as I struggled to keep my weight down, my spirits up, and some hair on my head. One day, after staring in shock at a big bald patch, I tore through my refrigerator like a white tornado, tossing out all foods that contained refined sugar and corn syrup.

Here's the healthy hair diet that the Swiss doctors recommended: I ate two bowls of soup a day, plus green, yellow, and orange, vegetables, onions, sweet potatoes, spinach, kale, and watercress salads, topped with a generous serving of salmon or turkey.*

As the weight began to fall off I added blueberries, raspberries, almonds, biotin, chocolate with 70% cocoa, grass-fed beef, and goat cheese. Over the next few months I lost fifteen pounds and my hair grew back, healthier than ever.

If, like me, you've read almost every diet book on the planet, you'll notice there's a common denominator.

"Don't cheat," those diet gurus warn us.

"Of course you must cheat," I say.

Eating is one of the greatest pleasures in life. Cheat wildly on your birthday, at a friend's wedding, or on a romantic getaway. If you want to look like a million dollars on your birthday and enjoy an amorous rendezvous at any age, the simplest anti-aging secret is to reduce your intake of refined sugar.

As a former sugar-holic, I now limit my Häagen-Dazs ice cream indulgences to the weekends. Whenever you feel like indulging, please don't beat yourself up with guilty thoughts like "I wish I hadn't eaten all those Godiva chocolates." Your guilt trip will cause even *more* stress in your body. Cheat with gusto, enjoy every bite, but promise yourself that you will get back on track tomorrow.

Last January I was cheating with gusto in Coconut Grove. Coconut Grove is my favorite place in Florida, as it looks just like it sounds. It's a magical, mystical Miami locale, filled with lush coconut palms, old walled mansions, and movie stars with well-developed taste buds. Even the local grocery stores are stacked with fine wines, gourmet cheeses, and connoisseur coffees from every corner of the globe.

This is grocery-store shopping with a difference! In Coconut Grove customers wear $200 designer jeans as they shop for Dom Pérignon and a dozen roses. It's certainly no surprise when they bump into famous football players and infamous movie stars, sampling Jamaican Blue Mountain coffee along with those exotic Hawaiian blends.

This was my run-away-and-hide weekend. I had spent the past year coaching clients who had career, relationship, or creativity blocks, and sometimes all three. I hadn't taken any time off in months, and my mind and body were weary.

It was my birthday and the *perfect* time to spend a long weekend with an old flame who had recently purchased a winter home in Coconut Grove. I tossed my sexiest jeans and my skimpiest tops into a suitcase and drove away at high speed to my secret sortie in the grove.

No, no, naughty, naughty – it's *not* what you thought. This wasn't a *sex orgy* weekend, this was a *food orgy* weekend!

My Latin-American host had never subscribed to sugar-free eating, in any way, shape, or form. Our mornings began with tiny cups of sweet black coffee, so caffeine spiked I was bright eyed and bushy tailed within seconds of my first sip.

Breakfast was a dish of chocolate-covered pastries served with pungent Panamanian coffee. The caffeine and sugar charge acted like a fiery rocket under my feet. Within seconds I was laughing loudly at his jokes and swimming laps in the pool like a human dynamo.

"Suzanna, you are becoming a true Latina," he said as he spooned sweet whipped cream into my black, syrupy coffee. My hands were shaking from the java jolt as I chomped on my second scrumptious pastry. My brain felt as if it was on sugar-coated speed as it was clobbered by the toxic cocktail of sugar, trans fats, and caffeine.

"By the way, I've invited a *New York Times* best-selling author to your birthday party. He's offered to write a review of your new book. Just like you Suzanna, he watches his sugars like a hawk. He hardly eats a thing when I invite him for dinner."

"Imagine that!" I replied.

My day continued to go downhill, nutritionally speaking. Alcohol was served with everything, including afternoon tea.

I decided to relax and stop worrying about my sugar intake for the weekend. "It is just a *weekend*," I said to myself, praying that I would be able to squeeze into my sparkly jeans on Saturday night.

Saturday night arrived along with fifty guests dressed in sexy, see-through outfits, and a lively Latin band.

Upstairs in my bedroom I was sucking in my stomach and holding my breath as I tried to wriggle into jeans that seemed to have shrunk a size overnight!

"How could I look so fat and bloated after *only* forty-eight hours of cheating?" I cried.

The truth sometimes hurts! I swallowed some pink Pepto Bismol to reduce the bloat before flinging myself on the bed to flatten my stomach. It was not a pretty sight! After feverish sweating, tugging and squeezing, I was able to close the zipper on my snug-fitting jeans.

I looked in the mirror and burst out laughing.

"I can't believe I gained so much weight in a *weekend*! I shouldn't have eaten all those pastries because these jeans are *so* tight." I tried bending down and immediately felt a sharp snap in the back seam.

"O lawdy," I agonized. "This could be my first X-rated birthday party. If I split the back seam, my booty will be exposed for everyone to see.

I imagined the review that the super-disciplined, *New York Times* best-selling author would write. British author, Suzanne St. George, binged on so many desserts at her birthday party that she split her jeans and shocked her guests by exposing parts of her anatomy that are best kept hidden by Victoria's secret.

I took a deep, calming breath before stepping onto the bougainvillea- covered balcony and staring at the dazzling Miami skyline. A golden moon was rising over the giant coconut palms, while below me, the lush tropical garden was filled with loud meringue music and shrieks of laughter.

Phew! I was relieved in more than one sense of the word as I loosened my zipper. Clearly *I* had no need to worry about being over-exposed. These glamorous Latinos were letting *everything* hang out. Flamboyant dancers were moving and shaking their voluptuous breasts and six-pack-abs beside the poolside bar.

I thought *my* jeans were tight but they were *baggy* compared to these heart-stopping outfits that left nothing to the imagination. Should I stare, or should I avert my eyes? After all, in England it's considered rude to stare. But it was hard to avoid these taut and well-toned bodies as they strutted their stuff for all to see.

"How do they do it?" I asked incredulously.

"Do what, *mi amor*?" my host replied.

"I know most of your friends have stressful careers, but they act as if they don't have a care in the world. What's their secret to staying so slim and sexy looking?" I asked

"Haven't you noticed that Latinos handle stress so much better than the rest of the world?" he replied. "We watch our British and American friends stressing over their jobs and bringing work home at the weekends. Latinos have a more laid-back attitude, so we leave our worries behind at the office.*

As he said the word "behind," he patted my derriere. "You look good in these tight jeans, Suzanna."

I wanted to giggle and say "Don't pat too hard as you are on very dangerous ground. If I make any sudden moves I could lose my dignity along with my jeans."

Instead, I acted as cool as my super tight jeans would allow and smiled.

"Look at you, Suzanna," he continued. "You arrived here looking worn out and weary from working too hard. Now you look so relaxed and happy. You should come to visit more often."

I wondered exactly how many food-orgy weekends it would take before I would have to swap my waist-slenderizing jeans for parachute-sized coveralls.

The next day, in the middle of a champagne brunch where the focus was more on the *champagne* than on the *brunch*, I received a phone call from an old friend and medical intuitive, Prometheus.

"How's your diet?" he asked. "You could gain weight really quickly this month, so I wanted to warn you to be especially careful."

"You are three days too late. I already broke all the rules!" I replied.

"I know this is a Sunday, but I want you to *abstain* from all caffeine, sugar, and alcohol," he said, completely ignoring my comments.

"Are you saying *never on Sunday*?" I laughed.

"As for caffeine, sugar, and alcohol, they've been my three major food groups for the past three days. How did you find out? Are you working for the Miami Vice diet police now?"

My food orgy weekend was no longer a secret, but how had I been outed? After all, I was in Coconut Grove, hidden away behind six-foot-high stone walls and silent coconut palms.

"Is this is how Princess Di felt when she tried to hide from the paparazzi?" I asked. "Whenever she planned a clandestine weekend away, she was always caught in the act!"

Prometheus chuckled. "Go ahead and enjoy yourself, and *don't* feel guilty about all that champagne and sugar as its your *birthday*. But be sure to get back on track tomorrow. Otherwise you will look like Carrie

Bradshaw in *Sex and the City* after too many Cosmopolitan cocktails — all puffy eyed and bloated."

"Thanks," I said, "I will."

RISKS AND REWARDS
TO LOOK YOUNGER AND LOSE WEIGHT

#1 If you want to lose weight, eat this.

Are you ready to lose some weight? Then eat more soup! Research shows that soup eaters lose weight and keep it off.*

To lose weight *and* fight the aging process, eat a variety of different-colored veggies. Each color denotes specific anti-aging phytonutrients that can slow down and even reverse the aging process.

"But anti-aging cooking is so time consuming, and I don't have the money for organic food shopping. Don't you have quick-and-easy recipes for busy people?" is a question I'm always asked.

The solution is to plan ahead. If you wait till you're ravenously hungry, you'll order a pepperoni pizza with a double order of french fries. This combination is guaranteed to have you reaching for the Nexium faster than you can say *New York deli*.

Here's my ten-minute, low-cal, high-fiber, healthy dinner recipe. I make a delicious stir fry with cauliflower,

broccoli, carrots, sweet potatoes, snow peas, mushrooms, and ginger. Sounds time consuming? Quite the reverse.
In Europe I love shopping leisurely for fresh fish and vegetables. In America, who has time for that? I buy big bags of frozen veggies and stir-fry them in a tablespoonful of coconut oil.* While they are still crunchy, I add some leftover turkey or fish, and voilà, my healthy dinner is ready in ten minutes.

On tired and hungry days, I'll add brown rice topped with sautéed mushrooms and a glass of sulfite-free wine, to soothe my mind, body, and soul.

#2 Wired or dog-tired most of the day?

If you answered Yes, you are not alone! Most of us living fast-paced lives are either one or the other.

Over 50 percent of us are so wired or dog-tired we have difficulty sleeping and get by on a few hours' shut-eye every night. Did you know that sleep deprivation is one of the primary reasons we pack on the pounds and age prematurely?* A lack of sleep causes our bodies to crave sugar, caffeine, and other stimulants. And so the cycle continues. . . .

If you have difficulty sleeping, I recommend Dr. Bach's Rescue Sleep.* This is made from English flowers and is a fabulous remedy for busy people whose brains won't switch off when they go to bed.

If you feel dog-tired, try the Bach flower Olive. If your energy has been depleted over the years from working too many hours or taking on too many

153

responsibilities, it may take several weeks until you feel like your old self again.

Olive is the best selling flower essence in England, because stressed out Brits have to deal with bad weather as well as their busy schedules!

Whether you feel wired or dog-tired, a twenty-minute creative walk will boost your brain power and burn off your stress. Why not take your creative walk in the evening so you can sleep more peacefully? (See chapter 6.)

I also recommend eating a dozen almonds (a natural source of calcium and magnesium) and wearing fluffy socks to bed. I *know* this isn't sexy, but fluffy socks will help you fall asleep faster and stay asleep longer.

#3 Reverse the aging process by stimulating both sides of your brain.

Most of us talk about aging and Alzheimer's in the same breath. "Alzheimer's disease begins thirty years before we are diagnosed," says scientist Dr. Paul Kenny, of The Scripps Research Institute in Florida.

What's the solution? Start taking better care of your brain today.

For years we've been told that our brain cells will die off after exposure to alcohol and chemical pollutants. Even worse, these precious cells could never be replaced.

The latest research shows that we *can* generate new brain cells by challenging our brains to study complex new projects and by exercising daily.

Why not challenge *your* brain to read the food labels on everything you eat? Chances are, if you can't understand the contents listed on the wrapper, your body can't process them properly.

Chemicals and colorants age us prematurely. Many chemicals and colorants permitted in foods in America are prohibited in Europe and Canada. It's no wonder we see so many ads for wrinkle creams on TV.

#4 Use a chlorine filter in your shower.

How we age correlates with the amount of chemicals we put into our bodies. Chemicals in our water supply can be absorbed through our skin. One solution is to use a chlorine filter. It attaches to the shower and costs about $50. Change the filter every six months for younger-looking skin and hair.

#5 Reduce your body burden!

I love New York. It's my favorite city in the world. After a couple of weeks in the Big Apple I feel totally exhausted. Its not from lack of exercise, or eating stodgy food. It's from all the smoke, exhaust fumes, and chemicals in the air.

Americans are exposed to over 80,000 chemicals and pollutants, and it's estimated that we carry 700 of these contaminants in our bodies. This is horrifically called our body burden.* Once our body burden reaches

155

overload, we get sicker quicker, have increased aches and pains, and age faster than our years.

If you live or work in the city, why not treat yourself to detoxifying ionic foot baths and healing foot reflexology.* This is a wonderful way to relax and reduce toxins in your body without removing your clothes.

#6 Balance your emotions with body mapping.

We inherited a genetic blueprint from our parents. This includes the color of our hair, eyes, and skin along with an emotional predisposition to being happy or sad. Studies show that babies born to depressed mothers are more likely to experience depression during their lives.*

Have you ever wondered why so many of us are unable to recover from food, alcohol, and cigarette addictions? Research shows that addictions have a genetic component. Whatever the cause, the recovery statistics are shocking. Less than 20 percent of us seeking professional help for our addictions will be successful in sustaining a long-term recovery.

As a recovery coach I am deeply troubled by these figures, especially as many of my family members were in that 80% failure rating. Even worse, addictions can lead to weight gain, premature aging, and life-threatening depression. I was on a mission to find simple, *natural* solutions to help them recover from their food, alcohol and cigarette addictions.

Here's what I discovered: While the genetic component remains, the emotional components that trigger these addictions can be reduced and often cleared for good.

In Germany, doctors who are experts in Bach flower essences, studied the effects of massaging individual flower essences into precise points on the body. It's similar to acupuncture without the needles. Using this non-invasive treatment, they were successful in reducing cravings and eliminating emotional blocks.

This treatment is called Bach body mapping and must be performed by a doctor or licensed massage therapist with expertise in Bach flowers and body mapping to ensure maximum success.

In England, Bach body mapping is often used in conjunction with hypnosis to speed up the recovery process. I used this powerful combination first on my family, and later on clients. I freely admit that my family's recovery successes surprised me. My family is from Yorkshire and Yorkshire folk are headstrong and resistant to change. Despite their resistance, many of them were able to quit long-term addictions through the combination of hypnosis, Bach body mapping, and manual lymphatic therapy.

#7 Reverse aging with lymphatic therapy.**

Did you know that the average life expectancy of an American man is seventy-eight years? Even worse, eight of those years are classified as unhealthy. While women live longer than men, they also have more unhealthy years.*

I find these figures *alarming* considering the mega-millions we spend on health care and anti-aging products to lengthen our lives.

Here's my #1 anti-aging secret. It works from the *outside in* and has been dubbed as the anti-aging secret of European royal families for decades. It's called lymphatic anti-aging therapy, or manual lymphatic drainage, and must be performed by a licensed massage therapist. The word "manual" is used to differentiate this life-changing, hands-on treatment from lymphatic suction machines.

Manual lymphatic drainage is a light and relaxing body treatment that removes toxins from the lymphatic cells. Congestion in the lymph cells affects our immune system and our ability to ward off infections and toxin-related issues that accelerate the aging process.

The treatment is so soothing that most people fall asleep during a session. In America it is now gaining wide acclaim, primarily through plastic surgeons, but we are still decades behind the times. In Europe and South America it's been used for almost a hundred years as a rejuvenation treatment following long periods of stress, and for pre- and post-op surgery to avoid complications, reduce scarring, and accelerate healing.

Manual lymphatic drainage is now being used successfully as an adjunct healing treatment for breast cancer and other cancers around the world.

Authors Note: I've treated two heads of state, award-winning actors, and world-famous athletes with manual lymphatic therapy in eleven countries, on four continents. This therapy successfully accelerated the healing and rejuvenation of their bodies after sports injuries or plastic surgery.

After twenty years' experience in this field, I'm still delighted at the effectiveness of manual lymphatic drainage in speeding up the healing process and resetting the body clock. Clients tell me they look and feel younger, as well as being mentally sharper, with reduced food cravings and increased sex drive.

I will leave the rest to your imagination. . . .

* See References and Research and St. George's workshop – Anti-aging Secrets from Around the World p.199.

CHAPTER 8

IS THERE A DRAGON IN THE HOUSE? ANGER MANAGEMENT ON THE HOME FRONT

TURN DRAGONS INTO DARLINGS BY TAKING RISKS IN LOVE

"The truth can set you free, but it can also drive you crazy."
- Suzanne St. George

"Are you happy?"

It's such a simple question, but when I ask it, most people will shake their heads and say, "Sometimes."

"How about your long-term love relationship? Is that happy?"

Talk about letting the cat amongst the pigeons! Typically I'll be subjected to a torrent of angry words: "I can't seem to do anything right these days. No matter what I say or do, all I'm told is I'm not making enough money, spending enough time with my family, or trying hard enough to lose weight."

"Sounds like you have a dragon in your house!"

In our fast-paced world, many formerly solid-as-a-rock relationships are facing a downturn, along with our finances. Over 50 percent of us are now wondering whether our relationships have been burned to the point where they are "beyond repair."

So what happened to those "I can't live without you" magical moments when you first met? Do you lie awake wondering why your relationship –which used to be so rapturous – now lacks passion, or even basic compatibility? Does it seem that you can't even *get along* anymore?

"Suzanne, is it possible to transform a love partnership that has lost all its passion and pizzazz?" people ask. "Our schedules are so busy that we never seem to have enough time for each other."

"Yes, yes, you can turn your relationship around, but it means taking *stimulating risks* in the love department.

"The secret to transforming your relationship has less to do with your hectic schedule and more to do with another kind of language that is simple and unspoken.

"No, it's not *sex*. It's your *body language*."

And to prove it, here's my own turn-around love story:

Years ago, before body language became a well-respected science, I was working in Central America and dating a man whose English was as flawed as my Spanish. When our language skills are limited, we have to resort to *body* language to express our wants and needs.

Have you promised to love each other in sickness and in health? Imagine having to fulfill that promise at a society wedding when you are struggling with a language barrier and your mate has the mumps!

I was one half of a fashion-conscious couple prepped and ready to attend the wedding of the year in Panama! If you watched the most recent royal wedding in London, you'll know that those posh guests didn't show up in just any old outfit. They spent weeks having custom fittings and eating colorless low-calorie foods to ensure that on the big day, their stomachs didn't stick out of their tight-fitting trousers.

I had been working out like a banshee, whatever a banshee is, so that every muscle in my body was sore. I may have looked good in my tight-fitting dress, but I ached all over.

After six weeks of eating low-carb, tasteless food and feeling voraciously hungry all the time, my attitude was less than *adorable* when my other half, Antonio, announced that he had the mumps!

"Can't go to ze wedding, Suzanna," he said. "My b@#s are too swollen!" His words were accompanied by several X-rated gestures that left nothing to the imagination, along with some comical facial grimaces.

"What do you mean you *can't go*?" I shrieked, repeating the same graphic gestures. "I've been working out and lifting weights for six weeks to lick my body into shape. *Please* say you're going!"

Antonio shook his head and stormed out. I took out my frustration on the treadmill and lived to regret it. While I had shapely glutes and hamstrings, it hurt like *hell* to walk.

Saturday morning arrived, and we boarded the flight in stony silence. Antonio wanted to be in bed drinking a hot toddy, while I wanted to be on a massage table having the kinks in my booty worked out.

Don't we sound like an *adorable* couple?

A limousine was waiting at the airport to take us to the wedding.

"I can't kneel," said Antonio. "My b@#s are too swollen!"

"I can't kneel either. My hamstrings are too tight!" I whispered.

So we sat at the back of the church — in silence again.

We arrived at the reception to find the bride and groom standing at the bottom of an ornate staircase. All the guests were gathered, watching the new arrivals walk down thirty steps to the reception hall.

This was the staircase from hell for both Antonio and me.

"Isn't there a back door?" he asked. "I can't go down ze staircase. Every time I take a step down my swollen b@#s get squashed."

My hamstrings were feeling the same way. But it was too late! The bride and groom were already signaling for us to descend. We were the stylishly dressed couple who couldn't *walk,* and couldn't even *talk,* without fighting. This was like a divorce scene from the show *Desperate Housewives.*

"Smile, you're on camera," I whispered, as a large video camera was pointed directly at us.

"Oh no," he groaned. "I'll never live this down."

He clung to one side of the railing, while I clung to the other. We hobbled in agonizing unison to the bottom of the staircase.

"What's wrong?" asked the groom, concerned about Antonio's pale demeanor.

Antonio muttered that he had the mumps, which meant his private parts were puffy and painful. The groom whispered back some choice words of comfort. Most likely it was the Spanish version of *gird your loins.*

"Thank you for coming in *that* condition," the groom said, giving Antonio a big slap on the back before glancing down to see if he could see any bulges in Antonio's slim-fitting pants.

"Stay right here and don't move a muscle," the groom announced in a commiserative tone.

That was easy, neither of us could!

Four throne-style chairs were carried in by the wait staff, and Antonio and I sat next to the bride and groom, as the *invalid* guests of honor.

Then magic happened! The band struck up an enticing salsa and all the guests leapt to their feet.

"Don't even *think* of asking me to dance," Antonio growled, waving me away dismissively.

But the music was so tantalizing, I quickly forgot about my sore hamstrings, and salsaed the night away with several handsome Panamanians. Surprisingly, the more I salsaed, the better my booty began to feel, and the more Antonio scowled furiously at me.

As the festivities wound down, word was spreading like wildfire that Antonio and I were no longer an *item*. He'd spent the entire evening hunched over in his chair and hadn't spoken a word or danced a single dance with me.

Caramba, I finally got it:

Frustration, pain, and anger had turned both of us into *dragons*. Antonio had a valid reason to be grumpy, while my pain was self-imposed. I had no training in simpatico body language, but it was clear that *one* of us had to take a risk and turn this relationship around, or we would soon be going our separate ways.

I put my arms around him and gave him a hug. "Amor, let's dance a slow dance, and then we can scoot out the back door while nobody's looking."

We swayed and shuffled to a sad love song until Antonio moaned "Ouch, *ouch*, watch out! You're pressing your tush against my tender b@#s!"

"Let's go," I sighed.

Antonio nodded appreciatively as we hobbled out the back door and headed for our hotel.

"OMG, did you book the honeymoon suite?" I gasped as I surveyed the champagne and roses in our room.

"That was *before* I had ze mumps," he growled. "And don't even ask! There'll be no hanky panky tonight, as you say. I have a *headache*."

I laughed. *Big mistake!*

"Really," he said indignantly, with his hands on his hips. "You have ze headache sooo many times, but I never laugh at *you*."

In body language terms, grinning or laughing at the wrong time can be very detrimental to your relationship. If you laugh because your date looks *fat* in her new dress, you'll be sleeping on the sofa with the dog for the foreseeable future. If you laugh because your mate has problems with his sexual performance, hell could freeze over before he approaches you again.

That night, as we eased our aching body parts with hot baths and arnica, I mused how the world had come full circle. In these days of equality of the sexes, men are now claiming a headache as an excuse!

Are you ready to take some risks and turn your dragons into darlings?

"OK, where do we start?"

Let's start by learning the secrets of body language.

If someone you love crosses their arms and legs, this signifies their desire to withdraw from you to protect their feelings from being hurt.

Instinctively, you feel rejected! But instead of shutting down and distancing yourself, why not try simple body language skills to bring you closer. All you have to do is cross *either* your arms or your legs in a loving, supportive gesture.

In body language you are saying *I understand and I care about you.* Isn't that what you wanted to say anyway but were afraid of being rejected if you did?

Take a deep breath, as I'm about to ask you to take another big risk.

If you are serious about reinventing your love relationship, you *must* be more attentive in the love department! I know, I know, for some of you this feels like too big a risk. For years you've been secure as the dominant partner in the relationship and resistant to doing things you consider romantically *ridiculous.*

You don't need me to draw you a graph, but if you stay open to meeting your lover's needs, this will show, rather than tell, that you are ready to rebuild your intimate relationship.

By now, some of you will be on the brink of throwing this book down in a fit of temper saying, "I'm too old, too tired and too fed up with my partner to fool around like that."

Here's the modern-day reality: If you're not ready to reinvent yourself as a loving and attentive mate, you may soon have to reinvent yourself as *single.* With the advent of the information age, there are a multitude of temptations available at the touch of a computer screen, and they are *not* just for singles. Now there are dozens of dating websites for bored-out-of-their-minds *marrieds.*

But what if your relationship isn't in dire straits? What if it's simply dwindled to a disappointing state of indifference? Do you secretly worry and wonder, "Is this as good as it gets for the rest of my life?"

If your relationship isn't working for any reason, you have only two choices: you can rebuild your love bridges or burn them!

The next risk is simple, but it can repair those love bridges and win you mind-blowing bedroom benefits for acting so attentively toward your mate.

It's not *what* we say, but *how* we say it that matters. "How on earth can this make a difference in my demanding relationship?" you may have wondered. Here's my secret recipe for creating romantic spoken rapport:

Imagine your voice is an electrical current. While we all use the same current, some of us need an adapter to get it.

If your partner is speaking on 200 volts (UK), and you are listening on 120 volts (US), there's a big disconnect! While the charge is always present, without a love adapter you might as well be speaking Martian for the amount they'll grasp.

It's time to plug in that love adapter and listen very carefully.

If your partner speaks slowly, then slow down as you respond. If they speak rapidly, then speed up your responses. This is not rocket science, but it works almost as fast. Yet all you are doing is adapting your *rate of speech* to be more in sync with theirs.

Now pay attention to your partner's *tone of voice*. If your mate speaks in a high or low tone, then raise or lower your tone slightly so you are on a similar vibration. That's it!

While it seems bizarre that making small changes to your body language and tone of voice can harmonize your love relationship, world-famous scientists have been studying this phenomenon for years. Dr. Masuru Emoto, the brilliant author and researcher, asks us to win without fighting by using harmonious vibrational resonance.

I demonstrate the extraordinary power of vibrational harmony at my book signings by using tuning forks. A tuning fork will only respond to another tuning fork that sends out a matching sound vibration. This happens even when there are hundreds of sleeker and sharper-looking tuning forks in the room. If you've wondered why some couples stay together even if they appear to be an unlikely match, now you know why!

Here's the absolutely fabulous outcome. As you become proficient in these sound and body language tips *your social life will become much easier, and your love life will become much happier.*

Unless you are a celibate monk, or have committed your life to a cause, most of us have spent years searching for ways to be *liked* more by our friends and coworkers and be *loved* more deeply by our mates.

So when I ask, "Are you happy?" Now, you can respond with a resounding "Yes."

"This is just a bunch of hooey. I'm much too busy for all this romantic b@# s@#," you may be saying.

Here's the dark and dastardly bad news. If you are unwilling to take a few risks to turn your relationship around, your beloved will assume you are bored with them. Before you can say, "Let's work it out," chances are they will have found stimulating sensual communication in someone else's arms.

RISKS & REWARDS
TURN DRAGONS INTO DARLINGS

#1 Safety is critical in our love relationships

Dr. Gary Smalley, a relationship expert, tells us that *safety* is a critical factor in any long-term love relationship.*

His words shook me to the core. I married a man with a terrible temper. Whenever he drank he turned into a fiery dragon. I played the role of peacemaker, instead of being myself. Most importantly, deep down, I never felt safe around him, and eventually I left.*

Are you are in a relationship with a dragon? Or, do you have a dragon-like temper? Know that *safety* is an underrated factor in any relationship. If you feel unsafe, sooner or later you must make the scary and gut-wrenching decision to leave.

Meanwhile, try these Bach flower essences for anger management on the home front.

- Holly – for jealousy and anger.
- Impatiens – for irritability and impatience with your mate.
- Centaury - for setting clearer, safer boundaries.*

#2 Am I missing something?

While most of us would say "I know *I'm* communicating clearly," the reality is that what seems clear to us may *not* be clear to our love partners.

Here are the most frequent questions I am asked about love relationships:

"We never had any problems before we were married. Why did our love fade, when we used to be so inseparable?"

"Why did he/she turn into a *dragon*? I gave up trying to understand and found someone new."

"Why does my best friend have a fabulous relationship, and I don't?"

My answer to all three questions is usually this: if you are unwittingly using an unlovable body language that belittles or affronts your love partner, sub-consciously they will feel neglected or rejected.

It's time to rethink your body language when you are with your mate. If you strut around the house wearing that tatty old T-shirt you walk the dog in, your dog may feel warm fuzzies, but your mate will not.

You are sending out a subtle message: "I don't care what *you* want. I'll do, or wear, whatever *I* want."

The outcome is your dog may want to sleep with you, but your mate will not!

#3 My mate never listens. . .

"He/she never listens to me," is the most common complaint I hear from couples who are drifting apart.

Are you familiar with the phrase, "It got lost in the translation?" This often applies to the tone of voice we use with our mates. As we try to translate the *vibes* in their voice into something we can understand we can miss something.

Here's a quick recap of my secret solution to show your loved ones that you're listening carefully, and most importantly, that you *really care*.

Pay attention to their speech patterns. If they speak slowly, then slow down your responses. If they speak rapidly, then speed up your answers so you are speaking with a matching sound vibration. Once you feel comfortable, raise or lower the tone of your voice *slightly* to be more in sync with theirs. That's it!

#4 Find compatibility in your handwriting.

We know that opposites attract, but too many "oppositions" can cause fights that lead to final good-byes.

Your handwriting is your *body language on paper*. You may be smiling at your mate, but if your handwriting reveals you are mad at them, what do you think they will feel? It's your anger, of course!

Did you know that handwriting is brain writing? When you consciously choose to make positive changes to your handwriting, it will have a positive effect on your emotions and your love life.

Let's say that you want to feel more optimistic. If you consistently cross the letter t with an upward stroke, this optimizes your positive outlook. This increased optimism will improve your attitude toward your partner as well as giving your love life an energy boost. (See Chapter 3).

#5 You tried it all, but nothing worked.

There's always a possibility, even if you pull out all the stops, that your lover will leave. If they can walk away and not look back, they were *never* truly committed to your relationship.

If this is your painful reality, how can you recover?

"Nothing is more important than feeling good," my mentor declared.

"*Exactly how* do you feel good when the love of your life is no longer around?" I asked.

"You sing," he replied.

You don't have to live in misery anymore. Here are three songs that worked well for me and many of my broken-hearted clients. "Owner of a Lonely Heart" by Yes, "Beat It" by Michael Jackson, and "Do You Feel Like We Do" by Peter Frampton.

After weeks of wailing to "Owner of a Lonely Heart," I felt so much better that I changed the word *lonely* to *loving*. No matter how lost and lonesome we feel, our hearts can still be loving and compassionate toward others less fortunate.

Frampton's "Do You feel Like We Do" has more whistling, clapping, and acoustic wailing than you can shake a stick at. It's impossible to feel sad and lonely when you sing along to this track.

Don't worry about your singing voice. Just do it!

#6 Love tips for lonely singles.
There's an interesting dichotomy in the world of dragons and darlings. Most of my single clients are

looking for *steamy sex,* and most of my married clients are looking for excuses to avoid it!

So what can you do if you are single, and steamy sex is not in the cards anytime soon? How can you make it through those long, lonely nights without someone to snuggle up to?

How about adopting a pet? With patience, you can find a special pet with a sense of playfulness and, yes, even a sense of humor.

While humans are said to be the only species with an ability to laugh, I would tend to disagree. My snooty Persian cat has a special laughing meow. *Mee yow,* she proclaims comically whenever I whinge and moan about my high-stress day.

In cat talk this means "Get a life." It certainly grabs my attention. It's impossible to take myself too seriously when clearly, in my cat's opinion; I need to have more fun.

Cats are the new aspirin. Cat owners have an unexpected benefit. Don't complain about that costly kitty food, because research shows that cat owners are less likely to have heart attacks than their catless counterparts.*

What if you are a dog lover? A run with your dog can burn off your stress faster than you can say "Kibbles 'n' Bits." Strolling in the park with an adorable puppy, whether it's yours or a friend's, is a fabulous way to meet new people and create new love connections.

#7 Creating closeness for two-career couples

It's time to switch off the stress response and switch on the love response. It's time to become the tender, loving person you always wanted to be, enjoying the tender, loving relationship that you always wanted to experience.

How many times did you laugh today? A four-year-old child laughs three hundred times a day, while a forty-year-old laughs only fourteen times.*

If you have a high stress job, you are probably wondering if you *ever* laughed fourteen times on a work day, unless it was at the office Holiday party, and you were a little tipsy.

How did we go from hundreds of laughs in our youth to double-digit laughter at midlife? It's called being *stressed out*.

Did you know that if you write the word "stressed" backward it spells "desserts?"

If there's drizzling rain after dinner, why not create a special dessert together? If the weather is clear, you could head outdoors for a stroll, followed by dessert in a café. One dish of low-calorie ice cream with two spoons can bring light-hearted fun and laughter to your relationship without demolishing your diet!

Laughter releases feel-good hormones called endorphins into our bodies. Endorphins are nature's way of keeping us healthy and happy. Promise yourself that you will laugh over dragons and desserts and grow closer as a couple, or as a family, every single day.

Transforming your love relationship means finding time for fun and laughter. Fun is the missing component that restores balance to our stress-filled lives. Fun and laughter bring healing to our work-weary bodies and our love-starved hearts and souls.

Loud outbursts of laughter can shift us from being "stressed-out" to being grounded and action oriented. Spontaneous humor soothes nerve-racking days and sleepless nights. Shared laughter with a loved one is the secret ingredient that makes even the toughest of days seem manageable and worthwhile.

Loving communication and laughter is the cement that patches up the holes that stress leaves in our lives. Best of all, it reinvents our love relationships—solid as a rock.

* See References and Research

Author's Note: Are you taking the right or the wrong risks in love? Laugh as you get the lowdown on taking the good, the bad, and the ugly risks in love, in St. George's third book, *The Naked Hello*, coming soon.

SIR FRANCIS DRAKE'S PRAYER 1577

Disturb us, Lord, when
We are too pleased with ourselves.
When our dreams have come true
Because we dreamed too little,
When we arrived safely
Because we sailed too close to the shore.

Disturb us, Lord, to dare more boldly,
To venture on wilder seas
Where storms will show Your mastery;
Where losing sight of land,
We shall find the stars.

Many of you reading this book will feel battered by life's storms. Not only have you lost sight of land, you have lost all hope of rebuilding your life, and making a fresh start.

At times like these, I invite you to try something that costs no money and takes very little time. Instead of feeling disappointment and even despair, why not take a couple of risks? Risks that can be as easy as dressing up on a drab and dreary day and smiling at complete strangers.

You don't have to sail the oceans and discover new lands to discover something new and daring within yourself. All I'm asking is that you raise the bar on *your* expectations.

Surely you don't want to get to heaven and have nothing to talk about. . . .

REFERENCES & RESEARCH

CHAPTER 1
GOOD MORNING PRIME MINISTER

Number 10 Downing Street is the official residence of Britain's Prime Minister.

Guy Fawkes attempted to blow up the Houses of Parliament with barrels of gunpowder on November 5, 1605. Wikipedia

November 5 is called Guy Fawkes Day in Great Britain and in most of the British colonies. Brits and ex-pats celebrate the rescue of their Houses of Parliament by burning effigies of Guy Fawkes on their backyard bonfires and by setting off fireworks.

Bobbies – Policemen in England are affectionately called Bobbies. They do not carry guns, which is why violent crime is less prevalent in England.

The Houses of Parliament is of made up of two chambers: the House of Commons and the House of Lords. Elected members of Parliament, including the Prime Minister, sit in the House of Commons. Earls, lords, and peerage sit in the House of Lords. Privileged members of the House of Lords host parties and wedding receptions at Britain's snootiest address.

Dying of a broken heart is called "broken heart syndrome" and is caused by overwhelming grief and sadness. Johns Hopkins University has conducted extensive research into broken heart syndrome. Dr Oz warns us that a broken heart can dramatically shorten our lifespan. DoctorOz.com

Emotional abuse occurs when a person's self-worth is undermined by controlling, humiliating and belittling behavior. Statistically 95% of victims of domestic violence involving emotional and physical abuse are women. Over 50% of American women will experience physical violence in an intimate relationship. For more information see WomensLaw.org - Am I being abused?

Union Jack News – A British newspaper published in America and enjoyed by many ex-pats. ujnews.com

Do You Dread Monday Mornings? How to be Resilient in a Stress-Filled world - Suzanne St. George's first book.

Stress and the City? Why use this title?
The statistics are startling:
82% of Americans live in cities
88% of Australians live in cities
72% of Europeans live in cities
79% of Brits live in cities.
The United Nations Percentage of Population Residing in Urban Areas...
Is it any wonder that we feel stressed living in such over-populated environments?

The Guardian newspaper reports that migration of the UK population to cities is projected to reach 92% by 2030. Guardian.co.uk.

While most of us live in cities, only 3% of the world's land mass is covered by cities and congested urban areas. Global Rural Urban Mapping Project.

William Keiper in his book *Life Expectancy: It's Never Too Late to Change your Game* reviews a study of ninety-five-year-old men and women and risk-taking.

An Adventure Board is a tool for activating the Law of Attraction. Learn how to create an Adventure Board in St. George's interactive workshops.

A recovery coach is a certified professional who offers caring support to clients dealing with all types of addictions.

Bach flower essences are English wildflower remedies and have been safely used in 60 countries for almost 100 years. They are preserved in small amount of alcohol. It is recommended you consult your doctor before taking any remedies containing alcohol.

Authors Note: Meredith Vieira, the smart and articulate anchor woman, spoke about the complexities of her abusive marriage, Sept 2014. A woman is abused every 9 seconds in America, she told her viewers.

CHAPTER 2
YOU LOST THE JOB AT HELLO

Nonverbal communication, such as body language and tone of voice, accounts for over 70% of our communication process states Professor Albert Mehrabian, author of *Nonverbal Communication,* 2007.

Switzerland is divided into twenty-six cantons. German, Swiss-German, French, Italian and English are spoken throughout Switzerland. Most Swiss nationals are multilingual.

Pride and Prejudice written in 1813 by Jane Austin reminds us how pride and prejudice is still alive, and not so well, one hundred years later.

The 80/20 Principle: The Secret to Achieving More with Less, by Richard Koch. The 80/20 principle also applies to our clothes! We wear 20% of our clothes, 80% of the time. From now on, why not spend your hard-earned money on the 20% that you wear the most?

J.B. Gossinger: MorningCoach.com

Jobs recovery is still years away for some cities – see USA Today article by John Waggoner, June 2013. Go to jobsreport.usatoday.com for a map of job market statistics.

Are you looking for a better job? Statistically 75% of the American workforce is looking to improve their job situation, so you are not alone! *Social Job Seeker Survey* Jobvite 2012.

Two of the top skills employers are looking for are good communication skills and flexibility. Wall Street Journal Nov 2012.

CHAPTER 3
WINNING OVER YOUR GREATEST FEARS

Public speaking is the #1 fear! *The Book of Lists;* WebMD.

Zip-lining is also known as the death slide – for obvious reasons! Steel lines are strung between tall towers and brave zip-liners are either strapped into harnesses before hooking onto lines that slide downward, or hang onto swings and jump - often with a drop of several hundred feet.

The Queen's Guards at Buckingham palace wear big bearskin fur hats, affectionately called busbies that become unbearably hot on a summer's day and can cause the guards to collapse from heat stroke.

Cortisol is known as the stress hormone as it is responsible for several stress-related changes in the body.

Rescue Remedy is a Bach flower essence for managing stress.

CHAPTER 4
WHO CAN YOU TRUST & WHO SHOULD YOU AVOID LIKE THE PLAGUE?

Graphology is the art of handwriting analysis.

Out of Africa, the award-winning movie starring Robert Redford and Meryl Streep is set in Kenya, East Africa.

Africa's Great Rift Valley is a 6,000-kilometer fissure in the earth's crust stretching from Lebanon to Mozambique. One of its most dramatic sections cuts through Kenya.

See the upscale Governor's Camp, Kenya, at GovernorsCamp.com.

CHAPTER 5
I'M LATE FOR AN IMPORTANT DATE

Time is the most commonly used noun in the English language. Wikipedia.

Bonnet is a British term for a car hood.

America works longer hours than any other nation. While 134 countries have legal limits to their workweek, America does not. *The International Labour Organization* states that each year the average American works 137 hours more than a Japanese worker, 260 hours more than a British worker and 499 hours more than a French worker.

In South Florida, roads over the intracoastal waterways can also be drawbridges. They open every hour or half hour. South Florida is not an ideal location to be late for a very important date.

Transcendental Meditation, or TM, was first introduced in India by Maharishi Mahesh Yogi in the 1950s.

The Mozart Effect: Tapping the Power of Music to Heal the Body, Strengthen the Mind, and Unlock the Creative Spirit. Author Don Campbell reviews Mozart's music as a tool for boosting brain function.

CHAPTER 6
THE CREATIVE WALK

The American Psychological Association states that 62% of Americans are affected by job stress, 66% of Americans suffer from a chronic stress-related health condition, and 50% of Americans consider their stress levels have increased.

Elizabeth Gilbert is the author of *Eat, Pray, Love.*

Dr. Laura Berman – a sex expert – states that stress negatively impacts our sex lives. drlauraberman.com

Stress and creativity researchers Mark Jung-Beeman a psychologist at Northwestern University, and John Kounios at Drexel University, found that walking is the best way to relax and stimulate our creative juices.

Walking helps improve memory. Participants in a study at the University of Western Australia who walked for 50 minutes 3 times a week showed positive improvement in both memory and cognitive brain function. These findings were published in the *Journal of the American Medical Association* in September 2008.

Labyrinth walk: To find a labyrinth near you go to Veriditas.org

Not taking time for a vacation? A Reuters report in September 2010 shows that over half American workers will not take all their vacation days, even though they need a break from their job stress. 64% of American workers admitted they had cancelled or postponed a vacation, often for work-related reasons. This is unlike British and French workers, who take all their allotted vacation time according to a 2012 *Vacation Deprivation* survey. Expedia.com

St. John was exiled to the Greek island of Patmos where he wrote the *Book of Revelation* in 95 AD. The cave where St. John lived and wrote the *Book of Revelation* sits on a hillside below a monastery. Visitors may enter the cave if appropriately dressed. Sacredsites.com.

Author's note: If you are interested in visiting ancient historical sites, this is one of my all-time favorites.

CHAPTER 7
ANTI-AGING SECRETS FOR CITY SLICKERS

Monday mornings are the high point in the week for heart attacks: See DoctorOz.com and *Do You Dread Monday Mornings?* Suzanne St. George's first book.

Is America the most medicated country on earth? The Department of Health and Human Services and the C.D.C.'s National Center for Health Statistics show that 48% of all Americans take at least one prescription drug, 75% of Americans over age 60 take two or more prescription drugs and most alarming of all, 22% of children under 12 take prescribed medication.

The use of antidepressants has tripled in the past thirty years – C.D.C.

How serious is depression globally? The World Health Organization predicts that by 2020, depression will be the second-leading cause of death in the world.

A recovery coach is a certified professional who offers caring support to clients coping with addictions. This spans food, alcohol and cigarette addictions that can damage our health, destroy our looks, and shorten our lives.

Sugar consumption hit an all time high in 1999, according to the US Department of Agriculture. The typical American ate 158 lbs - 30% more than in 1983. Imagine lifting fifteen 10 lb. bags of kitty litter and you can imagine what eating this amount of sugar will do to your waistline.

Dr. Oz tells us that sugar is the #1 food he wants to get out of your house. Sugar is linked to heart disease, high cholesterol, and diabetes. Sugar is public enemy number one when it comes to heart disease, says Dr. Stephen T. Sinatra, co-author of the book *Sugar Shock*.

The Gallup-Healthways Well-Being Index 2008/9 shows that of 62% of Americans are overweight. This is a dramatic increase from 48% of Americans overweight in 1980.

Soup can help you lose weight! Eating soup helps the stomach stay fuller for longer, staving off hunger pangs. news.bbc.co.uk.

Almost 90% of health issues are caused by stress, according to the American Medical Association.

The C.D.C statistics show that the number of Americans diagnosed with diabetes has tripled from 5.6 million in 1980 to 20.9 million in 2010. American Diabetes Association.

Ponce de Léon searched for the fountain of youth in Florida in 1513.

Coconut oil is described as "miracle oil" by Dr. Oz. Coconut oil helps with weight loss by firing up the metabolism so your body burns more calories and you feel fuller. Coconut oil improves the absorption of calcium and magnesium by the body for bone and dental health. Look for virgin coconut oil or organic coconut oil.

Latin-Americans are the world's happiest people according to a 2011 Gallup survey. Liveandinvestoverseas.com, December 2012.

What's your body burden? This is a buzz phrase for the number of chemicals and contaminants stored in the average body. See chemicalbodyburden.org.

Ionic detoxifying foot baths are offered by therapists who have been trained in anatomy, physiology, and foot reflexology.

A *Psychology Today* article in 2002 reveals that sad mothers can give birth to sad babies. Depression during pregnancy causes increased levels of the stress hormone, cortisol, and decreased levels of dopamine and serotonin.

Manual Lymph Drainage was introduced to Europe by Dr. Emil Vodder. It is highly effective in the management of immune disorders and chronic health issues. In Europe and South America, manual lymphatic drainage is used as an anti-aging treatment as it produces remarkable rejuvenating results. Positive outcomes include increased energy, mental clarity and reduced inflammation. Best of all, people using this therapy find they rarely get flu, and other debilitating illnesses and look years younger than their real age.

Manual Lymphatic Drainage is administered by hands, not machines, which is why the word *manual* is in the name. It must be performed by a licensed massage therapist. Top plastic surgeons now offer manual lymphatic treatments pre- and post surgery, to speed up their patients' recovery, with minimal scarring and bruising.

Bach flower body mapping is a body treatment for balancing the body's negative emotions safely and naturally.

CHAPTER 8
IS THERE A DRAGON IN THE HOUSE?

Divorce rates in America are 50% for first marriages and even higher for second marriages. Divorcerate.org

Gary Smalley is the author of *The DNA of Relationships*.

Who needs marriage? Men do more than women, according to *TIME Magazine*, November 2010. Men married to smart women live longer according to a 1990 Swedish census. The interesting factor in these men's longevity was the education level of their wives.

Happily married women cope better with career and family stress. After a tough day in the office, cortisol levels dropped lower in happily married women. Cortisol - the stress hormone - affects job burnout, depression, and family relationships. *Health Psychology,* the journal published the American Psychological Association, examined a study conducted by UCLA-Sloan Center on the Everyday Lives of Families, in 2008: Sciencedaily.com.

Live healthier with more laughter? *Psychology Today – "The Possibility Paradigm"* – June 2011. While the statistics vary according to each researcher, it is evident that children laugh hundreds of times a day, while adults laugh about fifteen times.

Cats are new aspirin! The University of Minnesota's Stroke Research Center completed a ten-year study showing that cat owners are 40% less likely to have a heart attack than their catless counterparts.

CURRENT PUBLICATIONS

DO YOU DREAD MONDAY MORNINGS?

How To Be Resilient In A
Stress Filled World.

Do you suffer from the Monday morning blues?

Do your Monday blues start on Sundays?

If you answered "Yes," it's time to read *Do You Dread Monday Mornings?* and learn tips and tools that will help you feel better on Mondays.

Here's what you will learn:
- How to prevent those Monday morning panic attacks.
- How to find the right job that's a perfect fit for you.
- How to deal with "fat" Mondays.
- How two words can improve your finances.
- How to take charge of your future and make your goals and dreams a reality.
- How to change the lives of 10,000 people in just 3 minutes a day.

To order copies of this book, and be placed on the mailing list, please go to **www.StressAndTheCity.com**.

STRESS AND THE CITY

The Power of Risk-Taking to Transform Your Life.

Have you been dumped by your lover, your long-term employer, or given a depressing diagnosis by your doctor? Are you burned-out by the stress of city life? It's time to take two risks a day and turn your life around.

Two risks a day will transform your life as you:

- Create your own miracles and discover your true purpose in life.
- Face your biggest fears and overcome them.
- Turn your dragon relationships into darlings.
- Instantly recognize someone you can trust from someone you should avoid like the plague.
- Turn back the clock with top anti-aging tips.
- If you'd rather milk a deadly cobra than face another job interview – take the right risks to get hired.

This book will take you from burned-out, to bright-eyed and bushy-tailed. Working in the city, whether you are in icy Alaska or sunny Florida doesn't have to zap all your energy. You CAN take back your power and start over.

THE NAKED HELLO

ARE YOU TAKING THE RIGHT RISKS IN LOVE?

The good, bad, and the ugly about taking risks in love.

- The naked first date. He's stark naked but she's fully dressed.
- Kidnapped in Venice! St. George's real life version of the Angelina Jolie movie.
- Ménage à trois in a haunted house in Maui. You've got to read it to believe it!
- Things that go bump in the night. To be or not to be a cougar?
- A lion in the loo? Do you sleep naked? You may change your mind after reading this.
- Boxers or briefs, or push-up bras and panties? It's not what you wear! It's the color that counts if you want to attract love.

St. George's third book will leave you laughing as you relish tips, tools, and exciting stories about taking risks for love around the world. "Am I romantically doomed?" she once asked. I've looked for love in all the wrong places, and had my heart broken so many times. Is it possible to find true love after making such bad choices?

Sounds familiar? This book is for you! Learn what's good, what's bad, what's really ugly in the world of romance and risk taking. Available soon...

BOOK SUZANNE FOR YOUR NEXT EVENT
OR CONFERENCE BREAK-OUT SESSION

Suzanne@StressAndTheCity.com

KEYNOTES & WORKSHOPS

ANTI-AGING SECRETS FROM AROUND THE WORLD

Did you know the body you woke up with this morning is not the same body you will take to bed?

Every day the type of food we eat, the quality of sleep we get, and the amount of stress we experience creates changes, good and bad, in our bodies. Wouldn't you like to wake up tomorrow feeling lighter and less stressed?

Learn what works and what's a fad in this lively entertaining program jam-packed with information and entertaining stories from around the world.

St. George researched the good, the bad, and the ugly, anti-aging foods and dieting trends for her second book Stress And The City while working on 4 continents.

Here's what you will learn:

- The 7 best foods to get you trim and healthy
- The 7 best ways to beat everyday stress
- What you put into and onto your body can age. or rejuvenate you. Make the right choices.
- Top budget tips to give you the best looks for your bucks

HOW TO WRITE AND SELF-PUBLISH A BOOK.

Have you always wanted to write a book?

Well now you can!

St. George takes you through her beginner's guide to writing and self-publishing jam-packed with entertaining stories and lively British humor.

Here's what you will learn:

- How to stimulate your creativity
- How to write like a professional
- The best time of day to be creative
- How to give yourself writing incentives
- How to deal with creative blocks
- How to choose your title
- Critical tools before you go to print, editing, ISBN bar codes and copyright

Laugh and be inspired by St. George's stories of her costly mistakes, rewards, and successes while writing three books so you can start writing *your* book today.

COURAGE & ADVENTURE
SKILLS FOR WOMEN

Are you ready to be more adventurous and courageous? Are you starting a new business, starting a new health and weight loss program, of starting over after your children have grown?

Welcome to an exciting new era of your life.

The courage and adventure skills in this program are based on Suzanne's St. George's second book, *Stress and the City*. Suzanne left an unhappy marriage to recover from her emotional eating disorder and find a sense of purpose for her life.

After years of being told she wasn't good enough, thin enough, or smart enough, she overcame her fears, worked in 11 countries, and wrote three books.

Suzanne's lively British humor brings her adventure stories to life and will have you laughing throughout her program. Her enthralling escapades will keep you on the edge of your seat and will inspire you to have more adventures in your own life.

Best of all you will learn the stress-coping skills Suzanne wished she had known before she was in the depths of the African jungle, the deserts of the Middle East, and the rainforests of Central America.

HOW TO BEAT THE
MONDAY MORNING BLUES.

Did you know that most heart attacks occur at 8:30 Monday morning?

Job stress costs employers $300 billion annually in US, in absenteeism, low productivity and employee turnover. That's more than all the net profits of the Fortune 500 companies combined.

A recent poll by Monster.com shows that 42% quit a job because of work-related stress.

This program is based on St. George's book *Do You Dread Monday Mornings?* It is packed with entertaining stories including her life-threatening encounter with Monday morning stress in Africa.

Here's what you will learn:

- Why the Monday morning blues start on Sunday
- Natural remedies for anxiety & panic attacks
- Tips and tools to beat the Monday morning blues.
- Job stress makes us fatter. How to look 10 lbs thinner on Mondays
- How to be in the top 10% and achieve your goals and dreams. (90% of us do not do this).
- How to be a successful risk-taker.
- How to touch lives of 10,000 people in 3 minutes a day.

HAUTE HEALING AND COACHING SERVICES

Suzanne St. George is a British author, speaker and stress management expert. She has worked with well-known sports stars, corporate leaders, and two heads of state, in 11 countries world-wide. Suzanne brings balance, stress reduction and rejuvenation to her client's minds, bodies and emotions. Her extensive training in holistic therapies and natural remedies ensures a haute healing, or optimum outcome to every session.

Manual Lymphatic Drainage - is a soothing and gentle body massage that detoxifies the lymphatic system. Lymphatic drainage has been used by European royal families for decades for rejuvenation and increased longevity. Lymphatic drainage is called the fountain of youth treatment by European health experts as it reduces stress-related inflammation in the face and body.

Manual lymphatic drainage is frequently recommended by plastic surgeons, pre- and post- surgery to speed up the healing process with minimal scarring. Patients undergoing chemotherapy and radiation are often prescribed lymphatic drainage to boost the immune system and restore energy naturally.

Ionic Detoxifying Foot Baths.
Did you know that we are exposed to over 80,000 chemicals and pollutants in America? Did you know that many of the chemicals in our food and personal care products are illegal in Europe and Canada? It's

estimated that Americans have 700 of these toxins in our bodies. This is horrifyingly called our body burden. Once our body burden reaches overload, we get sicker quicker and age prematurely.

Ionic foot baths draw toxins from the feet with harmless activators. As a skeptic, St. George was astonished at the amount of toxins she released after years living in polluted cities around the world. Many of St. George's clients in recovery from addictions and chronic health conditions found their energy levels increased and their cravings were dramatically reduced with the use of ionic foot baths and lymphatic drainage.

Foot Reflexology accelerates the cleansing process following a foot bath or lymphatic therapy. The foot has reflex zones that can reduce pain and recharge every organ in the body. It's a fabulous way to relax and de-tox without removing your clothes. Read Foot Reflexology success stories in St. George's book *Do You Dread Monday Mornings?*

Recovery & Health Coaching

We are all recovering from something! Whether it's the loss of a loved one, loss of a job, or money, or the loss of our health. The outcome can range from fear and anxiety to depression, panic attacks, and addiction.

Many of us find comfort in food and other substance to soothe our emotional pain. Sadly, all too often this ends up as an addiction and less than 20% will be successful in maintaining recovery. Recovery coaching explores the latest treatments and healing therapies while giving compassionate support to sustain a long-term recovery.

St. George battled a life-threatening emotional eating disorder when her marriage disintegrated. With the support of a recovery coach and the holistic therapies she now offers: - lymphatic drainage, foot reflexology, and natural remedies for stress, food addiction and fear, she made a complete recovery and now helps others with similar challenges.

Life Coaching

Did you know that only 10% of us will achieve our lifetime goals and dreams? What differentiates those who succeed, despite the odds, and those who don't? Surprisingly, it depends much less on learned skills and more on the motivating and sustaining support of a life coach! "My career was completely transformed by my life coach," says St. George. "He kept me on track when I wanted to quit and stuck by me when others said I'd never succeed."

St. George's life coaching gives practical tips and tools to help you stay on track and accomplish your goals, despite life's constant challenges and distractions

Suzanne@StressAndTheCity.com

About the Author

Suzanne is affectionately known as "Magic Hands" by her clients all around the world. As a British stress management expert, holistic therapist, and life coach, Suzanne travels internationally to give healing therapies, teach workshops and coach her clients in stress management skills. She has worked in Europe, Africa, North and Central America, India, the Caribbean and the Middle East.

Five years ago, when the man she was dating died from a Monday morning heart attack; Suzanne took some time to heal herself. "How is it that we can put a man on the moon, fly at supersonic speeds and yet we still haven't learned how to manage our stress?" she asked her mentor, an eminent British psychologist.

"I want you to see this time as a gift. The world has been waiting for you to heal with your words, as well as your hands," he replied. Five years later with two books published; Suzanne is busy writing her third.

"All of us will face losses in our lives; whether it's the loss of a job, loss of money, or the loss of people we love," Suzanne says. "When bad things happen to us, we can be stuck with those sad feelings for months, years, and sometimes the rest of our lives. My goal in writing these books is to help you laugh, learn and feel better no matter what is going on in your life.

Suzanne's favorite things are Hawaii, boating, strolling on the beach at sunset, art galleries, street cafés in Paris, and cooking delicious healthy dinners for her friends. Next year she plans to fulfill a life-long dream and visit Australia to search for her relatives who emigrated from England years ago.

Do you want to feel this relaxed on a Monday Morning? Be sure to read Suzanne's first book "Do You Dread Monday Mornings?" p.193 & take her workshop "How To Beat Monday Morning Blues" p.202